The Image

Ann Arbor Paperbacks   *The University of Michigan Press*

Knowledge in Life and Society

THE
IMAGE

by Kenneth E. Boulding

Tenth printing 1975
First edition as an Ann Arbor Paperback 1961
Copyright © by The University of Michigan 1956
All rights reserved
ISBN 0-472-06047-3 (paperbound)
ISBN 0-472-09047-x (clothbound)
Published in the United States of America by
The University of Michigan Press and simultaneously
in Don Mills, Canada, by Longman Canada Limited
Manufactured in the United States of America

Preface

THIS BOOK
is the result of the impact of a unique experience and a unique institution. I spent the academic year 1954–55 at the Center for Advanced Study in the Behavioral Sciences at Stanford, California, described by a perceptive Catholic priest as a retreat house for the intellect. Eleven months of vigorous interaction, both playful and serious, with a group of thirty-six able social and biological scientists produced in me a state of mind in which the following monograph was written, or rather dictated, in uninterrupted composition. My readers may therefore wish to discount, and even to forgive, a certain atmosphere of intellectual exaltation which inevitably pervades it and which no sober editing can quite remove.

I am sincerely grateful to the Director, the staff, and my colleagues at the Behavioral Sciences Center for creating the setting in which this work became possible, while absolving them from any responsibility for its errors and inconsistencies. I am grateful also to the Ford Foundation for daring to invest risk capital in intellectual enterprise. And I must not forget my daily bread, the University of Michigan, where the long groundwork for the present work was laid in my Seminar in the Integration of the Social Sciences and where the fruits, if any, must develop.

K.E.B.

Ann Arbor, Michigan, January 18, 1956

Contents

The Image

Introduction

AS I SIT AT MY DESK, I know where I am. I see before me a window; beyond that some trees; beyond that the red roofs of the campus of Stanford University; beyond them the trees and the roof tops which mark the town of Palo Alto; beyond them the bare golden hills of the Hamilton Range. I know, however, more than I see. Behind me, although I am not looking in that direction, I know there is a window, and beyond that the little campus of the Center for the Advanced Study in the Behavioral Sciences; beyond that the Coast Range; beyond that the Pacific Ocean. Looking ahead of me again, I know that beyond the mountains that close my present horizon, there is a broad valley; beyond that a still higher range of mountains; beyond that other mountains, range upon range, until we come to the Rockies; beyond that the Great Plains and the Mississippi; beyond that the Alleghenies; beyond that the eastern seaboard; beyond that the Atlantic Ocean; beyond that is Europe; beyond that is Asia. I know, furthermore, that if I go far enough I will come back to where I am now. In other words, I have a picture of the earth as round. I visualize it as a globe. I am a little hazy on some of the details. I am not quite sure, for in-

stance, whether Tanganyika is north or south of Nyasaland. I probably could not draw a very good map of
Indonesia, but I have a fair idea where everything is
located on the face of this globe. Looking further, I visualize the globe as a small speck circling around a bright
star which is the sun, in the company of many other
similar specks, the planets. Looking still further, I see our
star the sun as a member of millions upon millions of
others in the Galaxy. Looking still further, I visualize the
Galaxy as one of millions upon millions of others in the
universe.

I am not only located in space, I am located in time.
I know that I came to California about a year ago, and I
am leaving it in about three weeks. I know that I have
lived in a number of different places at different times.
I know that about ten years ago a great war came to an
end, that about forty years ago another great war came
to an end. Certain dates are meaningful: 1776, 1620, 1066.
I have a picture in my mind of the formation of the earth,
of the long history of geological time, of the brief history
of man. The great civilizations pass before my mental
screen. Many of the images are vague, but Greece follows Crete, Rome follows Assyria.

I am not only located in space and time, I am located
in a field of personal relations. I not only know where
and when I am, I know to some extent who I am. I am
a professor at a great state university. This means that in
September I shall go into a classroom and expect to find
some students in it and begin to talk to them, and nobody
will be surprised. I expect, what is perhaps even more
agreeable, that regular salary checks will arrive from
the university. I expect that when I open my mouth on
certain occasions people will listen. I know, furthermore,
that I am a husband and a father, that there are people

4

who will respond to me affectionately and to whom I will respond in like manner. I know, also, that I have friends, that there are houses here, there, and everywhere into which I may go and I will be welcomed and recognized and received as a guest. I belong to many societies. There are places into which I go, and it will be recognized that I am expected to behave in a certain manner. I may sit down to worship, I may make a speech, I may listen to a concert, I may do all sorts of things.

I am not only located in space and in time and in personal relationships, I am also located in the world of nature, in a world of how things operate. I know that when I get into my car there are some things I must do to start it; some things I must do to back out of the parking lot; some things I must do to drive home. I know that if I jump off a high place I will probably hurt myself. I know that there are some things that would probably not be good for me to eat or to drink. I know certain precautions that are advisable to take to maintain good health. I know that if I lean too far backward in my chair as I sit here at my desk, I will probably fall over. I live, in other words, in a world of reasonably stable relationships, a world of "ifs" and "thens," of "if I do this, then that will happen."

Finally, I am located in the midst of a world of subtle intimations and emotions. I am sometimes elated, sometimes a little depressed, sometimes happy, sometimes sad, sometimes inspired, sometimes pedantic. I am open to subtle intimations of a presence beyond the world of space and time and sense.

What I have been talking about is knowledge. Knowledge, perhaps, is not a good word for this. Perhaps one would rather say my *Image* of the world. Knowledge has an implication of validity, of truth. What I am talking about is what I believe to be true; my subjective knowledge. It is this Image that largely governs my behavior. In about an hour I shall rise, leave my office, go to a car, drive down to my home, play with the children, have supper, perhaps read a book, go to bed. I can predict this behavior with a fair degree of accuracy because of the knowledge which I have: the knowledge that I have a home not far away, to which I am accustomed to go. The prediction, of course, may not be fulfilled. There may be an earthquake, I may have an accident with the car on the way home, I may get home to find that my family has been suddenly called away. A hundred and one things may happen. As each event occurs, however, it alters my knowledge structure or my image. And as it alters my image, I behave accordingly. *The first proposition of this work, therefore, is that behavior depends on the image.*

What, however, determines the image? This is the central question of this work. It is not a question which can be answered by it. Nevertheless, such answers as I shall give will be quite fundamental to the understanding of how both life and society really operate. One thing is clear. The image is built up as a result of all past experience of the possessor of the image. Part of the image is the history of the image itself. At one stage the image, I suppose, consists of little else than an undifferentiated blur and movement. From the moment of birth if not before, there is a constant stream of messages entering the organism from the senses. At first, these may merely be undifferentiated lights and noises. As the child grows, however, they gradually become distinguished into people and objects. He begins to perceive himself as an object in the midst of a world of objects. The conscious image has begun. In infancy the world is a house and, perhaps, a few streets or a park. As the child grows his

6

image of the world expands. He sees himself in a town, a country, on a planet. He finds himself in an increasingly complex web of personal relationships. Every time a message reaches him his image is likely to be changed in some degree by it, and as his image is changed his behavior patterns will be changed likewise.

We must distinguish carefully between the image and the messages that reach it. The messages consist of *information* in the sense that they are structured experiences. *The meaning of a message is the change which it produces in the image.*

When a message hits an image one of three things can happen. In the first place, the image may remain unaffected. If we think of the image as a rather loose structure, something like a molecule, we may imagine that the message is going straight through without hitting it. The great majority of messages is of this kind. I am receiving messages all the time, for instance, from my eyes and my ears as I sit at my desk, but these messages are ignored by me. There is, for instance, a noise of carpenters working. I know, however, that a building is being built nearby and the fact that I now hear this noise does not add to this image. Indeed, I do not hear the noise at all if I am not listening for it, as I have become so accustomed to it. If the noise stops, however, I notice it. This information changes my image of the universe. I realize that it is now five o'clock, and it is time for me to go home. The message has called my attention, as it were, to my position in time, and I have re-evaluated this position. This is the second possible effect or impact of a message on an image. It may change the image in some rather regular and well-defined way that might be described as simple addition. Suppose, for instance, to revert to an earlier illustration, I look at an atlas and find out exactly the relation of Nyasaland to Tanganyika. I will have added to my knowledge, or my image; I will not, however, have very fundamentally revised it. I still picture the world much as I had pictured it before. Something that was a little vague before is now clearer.

There is, however, a third type of change of the image which might be described as a revolutionary change. Sometimes a message hits some sort of nucleus or supporting structure in the image, and the whole thing changes in a quite radical way. A spectacular instance of such a change is conversion. A man, for instance, may think himself a pretty good fellow and then may hear a preacher who convinces him that, in fact, his life is worthless and shallow, as he is at present living it. The words of the preacher cause a radical reformulation of the man's image of himself in the world, and his behavior changes accordingly. The psychologist may say, of course, that these changes are smaller than they appear, that there is a great mass of the unconscious which does not change, and that the relatively small change in behavior which so often follows intellectual conversion is a testimony to this fact. Nevertheless, the phenomenon of reorganization of the image is an important one, and it occurs to all of us and in ways that are much less spectacular than conversion.

The sudden and dramatic nature of these reorganizations is perhaps a result of the fact that our image is in itself resistant to change. When it receives messages which conflict with it, its first impulse is to reject them as in some sense untrue. Suppose, for instance, that somebody tells us something which is inconsistent with our picture of a certain person. Our first impulse is to reject the proffered information as false. As we continue to receive

8

messages which contradict our image, however, we begin to have doubts, and then one day we receive a message which overthrows our previous image and we revise it completely. The person, for instance, whom we saw as a trusted friend is now seen to be a hypocrite and a deceiver.

Occasionally, things that we see, or read, or hear, revise our conceptions of space and time, or of relationships. I have recently read, for instance, Vasiliev's *History of the Byzantine Empire*. As a result of reading this book I have considerably revised my image of at least a thousand years of history. I had not given the matter a great deal of thought before, but I suppose if I had been questioned on my view of the period, I would have said that Rome fell in the fifth century and that it was succeeded by a little-known empire centering in Constantinople and a confused medley of tribes, invasions, and successor states. I now see that Rome did not fall, that in a sense it merely faded away, that the history of the Roman Empire and of Byzantium is continuous, and that from the time of its greatest extent the Roman Empire lost one piece after another until only Constantinople was left; and then in 1453 that went. There are books, some of them rather bad books, after which the world is never quite the same again. Veblen, for instance, was not, I think, a great social scientist, and yet he invented an undying phrase: "conspicuous consumption." After reading Veblen, one can never quite see a university campus or an elaborate house in just the same light as before. In a similar vein, David Riesman's division of humanity into inner-directed and other-directed people is no doubt open to serious criticism by the methodologists. Nevertheless, after reading Riesman one has a rather

9

new view of the universe and one looks in one's friends and acquaintances for signs of inner-direction or other-direction.

One should perhaps add a fourth possible impact of the messages on the image. The image has a certain dimension, or quality, of certainty or uncertainty, probability or improbability, clarity or vagueness. Our image of the world is not uniformly certain, uniformly probable, or uniformly clear. Messages, therefore, may have the effect not only of adding to or of reorganizing the image. They may also have the effect of clarifying it, that is, of making something which previously was regarded as less certain more certain, or something which was previously seen in a vague way, clearer.

Messages may also have the contrary effect. They may introduce doubt or uncertainty into the image. For instance, the noise of carpenters has just stopped, but my watch tells me it is about four-thirty. This has thrown a certain amount of confusion into my mental image. I was under the impression that the carpenters stopped work at five o'clock. Here is a message which contradicts that impression. What am I to believe? Unfortunately, there are two possible ways of integrating the message into my image. I can believe that I was mistaken in thinking that the carpenters left work at five o'clock and that in fact their day ends at four-thirty. Or, I can believe that my watch is wrong. Either of these two modifications of my image gives meaning to the message. I shall not know for certain which is the right one, however, until I have an opportunity of comparing my watch with a timepiece or with some other source of time which I regard as being more reliable.

The impact of messages on the certainty of the image is of great importance in the interpretation of human behavior. Images of the future must be held with a degree of uncertainty, and as time passes and as the images become closer to the present, the messages that we receive inevitably modify them, both as to content and as to certainty.

The subjective knowledge structure or image of any individual or organization consists not only of images of "fact" but also images of "value." We shall subject the concept of a "fact" to severe scrutiny in the course of the discussion. In the meantime, however, it is clear that there is a certain difference between the image which I have of physical objects in space and time and the valuations which I put on these objects or on the events which concern them. It is clear that there is a certain difference between, shall we say, my image of Stanford University existing at a certain point in space and time, and my image of the value of Stanford University. If I say "Stanford University is in California," this is rather different from the statement "Stanford University is a good university, or is a better university than X, or a worse university than Y." The latter statements concern my image of values, and although I shall argue that the process by which we obtain an image of values is not very different from the process whereby we obtain an image of fact, there is clearly a certain difference between them.

The image of value is concerned with the *rating* of the various parts of our image of the world, according to some scale of betterness or worseness. We, all of us, possess one or more of these scales. It is what the economists call a welfare function. It does not extend over the whole universe. We do not now, for instance, generally regard Jupiter as a better planet than Saturn. Over that part of the universe which is closest to ourselves, however, we all erect these scales of valuation. Moreover, we change these scales of valuation in response to messages received much as we change our image of the world around us. It is almost certain that most people possess not merely one scale of valuation but many scales for different purposes. For instance, we may say A is better than B for me but worse for the country, or it is better for the country but worse for the world at large. The notion of a hierarchy of scales is very important in determining the effect of messages on the scales themselves.

One of the most important propositions of this theory is that the value scales of any individual or organization are perhaps the most important single element determining the effect of the messages it receives on its image of the world. If a message is perceived that is neither good nor bad it may have little or no effect on the image. If it is perceived as bad or hostile to the image which is held, there will be resistance to accepting it. This resistance is not usually infinite. An often repeated message or a message which comes with unusual force or authority is able to penetrate the resistance and will be able to alter the image. A devout Moslem, for instance, whose whole life has been built around the observance of the precepts of the Koran will resist vigorously any message which tends to throw doubt on the authority of his sacred work. The resistance may take the form of simply ignoring the message, or it may take the form of emotive response: anger, hostility, indignation. In the same way, a "devout" psychologist will resist strongly any evidence presented in favor of extrasensory perception, because to accept it would overthrow his whole image of the universe. If the resistances are very strong, it may take very strong, or often repeated messages to penetrate them, and when they are penetrated, the effect is a realignment or reorganization of the whole knowledge structure.

On the other hand, messages which are favorable to the existing image of the world are received easily and even though they may make minor modifications of the knowledge structure, there will not be any fundamental reorganization. Such messages either will make no impact on the knowledge structure or their impact will be one of rather simple addition or accretion. Such messages may also have the effect of increasing the stability, that is to say, the resistance to unfavorable messages, which the knowledge structure or image possesses.

The stability or resistance to change of a knowledge structure also depends on its internal consistency and arrangement. There seems to be some kind of principle of minimization of internal strain at work which makes some images stable and others unstable for purely internal reasons. In the same way, some crystals or molecules are more stable than others because of the minimization of internal strain. It must be emphasized that it is not merely logical consistency which gives rise to internal cohesiveness of a knowledge structure, although this is an important element. There are important qualities of a nonlogical nature which also give rise to stability. The structure may, for instance, have certain aesthetic relationships among the parts. It may represent or justify a way of life or have certain consequences which are highly regarded in the value system, and so on. Even in mathematics, which is of all knowledge structures the one whose internal consistency is most due to logic, is not devoid of these nonlogical elements. In the acceptance of mathematical arguments by mathematicians there are important criteria of elegance, beauty, and simplicity which contribute toward the stability of these structures.

Even at the level of simple or supposedly simple sense perception we are increasingly discovering that the message which comes through the senses is itself mediated through a value system. We do not perceive our sense data raw; they are mediated through a highly learned process of interpretation and acceptance. When an object apparently increases in size on the retina of the eye, we interpret this not as an increase in size but as movement. Indeed, we only get along in the world because we consistently and persistently disbelieve the plain evidence of our senses. The stick in water is not bent; the movie is not a succession of still pictures; and so on.

What this means is that for any individual organism or organization, there are no such things as "facts." There are only messages filtered through a changeable value system. This statement may sound rather startling. It is inherent, however, in the view which I have been propounding. This does not mean, however, that the image of the world possessed by an individual is a purely private matter or that all knowledge is simply subjective knowledge, in the sense in which I have used the word. Part of our image of the world is the belief that this image is shared by other people like ourselves who also are part of our image of the world. In common daily intercourse we all behave as if we possess roughly the same image of the world. If a group of people are in a room together, their behavior clearly shows that they all think they are in the same room. It is this shared image which is "public" knowledge as opposed to "private" knowledge. It follows, however, from the argument above that if a group of people are to share the same image of the world, or to put it more exactly, if the various images of the world which they have are to be roughly identical, and if this group of people are exposed to much the same set of messages in building up images of the world, the value systems of all individuals must be approximately the same.

The problem is made still more complicated by the fact that a group of individuals does not merely share messages which come to them from "nature." They also initiate and receive messages themselves. This is the characteristic which distinguishes man from the lower organisms—the art of conversation or discourse. The human organism is capable not only of having an image of the world, but of talking about it. This is the extraordinary gift of language. A group of dogs in a pack pursuing a stray cat clearly share an image of the world in the sense that each is aware to some degree of the situation which they are all in, and is likewise aware of his neighbors. When the chase is over, however, they do not, as far as we know, sit around and talk about it and say, "Wasn't that a fine chase?" or, "Isn't it too bad the cat got away?" or even, "Next time you ought to go that way and I'll go this way and we can corner it." It is discourse or conversation which makes the human image public in a way that the image of no lower animal can possibly be. The term, "universe of discourse" has been used to describe the growth and development of common images in conversation and linguistic intercourse. There are, of course, many such universes of discourse, and although it is a little awkward to speak of many universes, the term is well enough accepted so that we may let it stay.

Where there is no universe of discourse, where the image possessed by the organism is purely private and cannot be communicated to anyone else, we say that the person is mad (to use a somewhat old-fashioned term). It must not be forgotten, however, that the discourse must be received as well as given, and that whether it is received or not depends upon the value system of the recipient. This means that insanity is defined differently from one culture to another because of these differences in value systems and that the schizophrenic of one culture may well be the shaman or the prophet of another.

Up to now I have sidestepped and I will continue to sidestep the great philosophical arguments of epistemology. I have talked about the image. I have maintained that images can be public as well as private, but I have not discussed the question as to whether images are *true* and how we know whether they are true. Most epistemological systems seek some philosopher's stone by which statements may be tested in order to determine their "truth," that is, their correspondence to outside reality. I do not claim to have any such philosopher's stone, not even the touchstone of science. I have, of course, a great respect for science and scientific method—for careful observation, for planned experience, for the testing of hypotheses and for as much objectivity as semirational beings like ourselves can hope to achieve. In my theoretical system, however, the scientific method merely stands as one among many of the methods whereby images change and develop. The development of images is part of the culture or the subculture in which they are developed, and it depends upon all the elements of that culture or subculture. Science is a subculture among subcultures. It can claim to be useful. It may claim rather more dubiously to be good. It cannot claim to give validity.

In summation, then, my theory might well be called an organic theory of knowledge. Its most fundamental proposition is that knowledge is what somebody or something knows, and that without a knower, knowledge is an absurdity. Moreover, I argue that the growth of knowledge is the growth of an "organic" structure. I am not suggesting here that knowledge is simply an arrangement of neuronal circuits or brain cells, or something of that kind. On the question of the relation between the physical and chemical structure of an organism and its knowledge structure, I am quite prepared to be agnostic. It is, of course, an article of faith among physical scientists that there must be somewhere a one-to-one correspondence between the structures of the physical body and the structures of knowledge. Up to now, there is nothing like empirical proof or even very good evidence for this hypothesis. Indeed, what we know about the brain suggests that it is an extraordinarily unspecialized and, in a sense, unstructured object; and that if there is a physical and chemical structure corresponding to the knowledge structure, it must be of a kind which at present we do not understand. It may be, indeed, that the correspondence between physical structure and mental structure is something that we will never be able to determine because of a sort of "Heisenberg principle" in the investigation of these matters. If the act of observation destroys the thing observed, it is clear that there is a fundamental obstacle to the growth of knowledge in that direction.

All these considerations, however, are not fundamental to my position. We do not have to conceive of the knowledge structure as a physico-chemical structure in order to use it in our theoretical construct. It can be inferred from the behavior of the organism just as we constantly infer the images of the world which are possessed by those around us from the messages which they transmit to us. When I say that knowledge is an organic structure, I mean that it follows principles of growth and development similar to those with which we are familiar in complex organizations and organisms. In every organism or organization there are both internal and external factors affecting growth. Growth takes place through a kind of metabolism. Even in the case of knowledge structures, we have a certain intake and output of messages. In the knowledge structure, however, there are important violations of the laws of conservation. The accumulation of knowledge is not merely the difference between messages taken in and messages given out. It is not like a reservoir; it is rather an organization which grows through an active internal organizing principle much as the gene is a principle or entity organizing the growth of bodily structures. The gene, even in the physico-chemical sense may be thought of as an inward teacher imposing its own form and "will" on the less formed matter around it. In the growth of images, also, we may suppose similar models. Knowledge grows also because of inward teachers as well as outward messages. As every good teacher knows, the business of teaching is not that of penetrating the student's defenses with the violence or loudness of the teacher's messages. It is, rather, that of co-operating with the student's own inward teacher whereby the student's image may grow in conformity with that of his outward teacher. The existence of public knowledge depends, therefore, on certain basic similarities among men. It is literally because we are of one "blood," that is, genetic constitution, that we are able to communicate with each other. We cannot talk to the ants or bees; we cannot hold conversations with them, although in a very real sense they communicate to us. It is the purpose of this work, therefore, to discuss the growth of images, both private and public, in individuals, in organizations, in society at large, and even with some trepidation, among the lower forms of life. Only thus can we develop a really adequate theory of behavior.

2

The Image in the Theory of Organization

IN THE IMAGE of the history of the universe, as it is presented to us by science, two opposing forces, or tendencies, seem to be operating. On the one hand, we have the tendency represented by the second law of thermodynamics; the tendency, that is, for states to become more probable, more chaotic, and for things to run down. The dynamics of the universe continually eliminates those differences in potential which give rise to movement or change. Heat-flows eliminate temperature differences; electric currents eliminate potential differences; the movement of matter eliminates gravitational differences. The end of the universe, according to this picture, will be a thin uniform soup without form. It is toward this comfortless end that all physical processes are moving.

On the other hand, we clearly observe in the record of history a different tendency. This is the tendency for the rise of organization. Organization is anything that is not chaos, anything, in other words, that is improbable. It consists of structures. In the course of the history of the universe, we observe the record of continually increasing complexity of organization culminating at the present day in man and his societies.

19

Many levels of organization can be distinguished. At the simplest level we have what might be called static structures: the jig-saw puzzle, the statue, the picture, and at certain levels of abstraction, the atom and the molecule are examples of this level of organization. These static structures occur in all fields of discourse. We have, for instance, the structural formula of the chemist; we have the structures described by the anatomists in biology. We have works of art, organization charts, and so on, in society. The world of static structures is the world of things, trees, houses, factories, roads, bodies, planets.

The next level of organization might be described as the level of the "clockwork." This is the level of the predetermined dynamic structure repeating its movements because of some simple law of connectedness among its parts. The great clock, of course, is the solar system itself, endlessly repeating its complex motions in the majestic wheel of the firmament. This is the world of mechanics. It is governed in the small by Newton's Mozartian equations; it is governed in the large by Einstein's atonal system. This is the universe of the eighteenth-century deists—wound up by the great Clock-maker in the beginning and unwinding ever since.

At the third level of organization, we have "thermostats": homeostatic control mechanisms. The theory of these mechanisms has only recently been worked out and is developed in the new science of cybernetics. It is at this point in the development of organization that the information concept becomes important. Consider for a moment how a thermostat operates. It consists essentially of three parts: a *receptor* (the thermometer on the wall), a *control* (at the furnace), and an *effector* (the furnace and the pipes which lead from it). The receptor has the property that it can detect a divergence, positive or negative, between the temperature recorded in its thermometer and some "ideal" temperature at which the thermostat is set. A channel of communication (which in this simple case need be capable only of one bit of information, that is, it can say either yes or no) feeds from the receptor to a control mechanism. If the message says "minus," that is to say, if the recorded temperature is less than the ideal, the control interprets this and sends out a message to the furnace which does, in effect, turn on the heat. If the message from the receptor is "plus," that is, if the recorded temperature is greater than the ideal, the message is interpreted by the control and another message goes out to the furnace saying, "turn off the heat." If these messages to the furnace are effective and if, when the furnace receives the "turn on" message, heat is sent up into the house, the "minus" message from the receptor results in an increase in temperature which eventually cancels the message. The same operation in reverse will cancel the "plus" message. This is what is meant by a "feedback."

Control mechanisms of this kind are very common. We find them, as a matter of fact, even in the clock—which is not pure clockwork. The pendulum or the spring is a control mechanism controlling the speed of the arms. It slows the clock down when it is going too fast, and it speeds it up when it is going too slow. The governor of a steam engine acts in much the same way. At the biological level there are innumerable such mechanisms. The word given by the great physiologist, Cannon, to the mechanism which permitted the biological organisms to maintain steady states or equilibrium values of its important variables in the face of changing environments, was *homeostasis*. The animal body can be interpreted largely as a device for insuring a constant internal environment for those parts of the structure which are most essential to its continual existence. The temperature and the chemical composition of the blood, for instance, are regulated by many subtle devices, all of them, however, analogous to the humble thermostat.

In a sense, we may say that the concept of the "image" begins in a very rudimentary form at this level. The thermostat has an image of the outside world in the shape of the information regarding its temperature. It has also a value system in the sense of the ideal temperature at which it is set. Its behavior is directed toward the receipt of information which will bring its image and its value system together. When its image of the outside world is "right," that is, conforms to its value system, it ceases to act. As long as the image, as confirmed by the messages received, does not conform to its value system it acts in order to bring the two together. Here, therefore, even below the biological level we see a concept something like that of the image in operation.

Moving now to the biological level, the next stage of organization is that of the cell. There may be a stage intermediate between that of the controlled mechanism and the cell, namely the complex molecule or virus. So little is known, however, about the operation of these structures that for the purposes of this discussion, they may be neglected. We shall regard the cell, therefore, as the simplest unit of life. It is characterized by many little control mechanisms and a quite elaborate internal structure. It differs from the nonliving control mechanism, however, in that it is an "open system," that is to say, as we shall see more clearly in the next chapter, it maintains its structure in the midst of a "through-put" of chemical material. It is not merely a homeostatic control system, it is a self-maintaining system capable of metabolism and digestion, that is, the intake of substances which it uses in part to maintain or to extend its own structure and which in part it rejects as excrement. In the cell the capacity for the receipt of information and the image which these messages construct is much more elaborate than in the simple control mechanism. Its view of the universe does not, of course, extend far beyond its immediate environment. Nevertheless, its behavior cannot be understood unless we assume that in some sense it has "knowledge" of its environment—that it interprets the information which it receives into the form of a knowledge structure. The cell is also capable of reproduction by division. It is capable of dividing itself into two parts each of which reproduces exactly the structure of the original cell.

Again passing over the intermediate forms of the molds and slimes, we come to the fifth stage of organization: the botanical level. A plant is a society of cells with a quite elaborate structure and extensive division of labor; that is to say, within a single plant there is a variety of cells, indeed a variety of cell societies, each of which receives something from the others and gives something to the others in a way that supports the continued existence of them all. The roots draw water and nutrients from the soil, but if these are not passed on to the rest of the plant, the root dies. The plant receives these substances and transforms them into a variety of forms and substances: trunks, stems, leaves, flowers, seeds. It is at this point that sexual reproduction becomes important, although it is not unknown even at the cellular level. The behavior of plants, like that of one-celled animals, can only be explained on the assumption that they build the messages which they received from their environment into an image of a simple kind. The plant "knows" when it is time to put out its leaves, to flower, to fruit, and to die. It has a time sense which includes, at least, the round of the seasons. It has "know how" in the sense of an ability to develop in an orderly manner from the seed, to the plant, to the seed again. "First the blade and then the ear and then the full corn doth appear."

Rising now to the sixth level of organization, that of the animal—again with some possible intermediate stages—we find here not only cell societies with division of labor, structural growth, and rudimentary images of time, we now have cell societies with something like awareness and mobility, differentiation of sleep and waking, and perhaps even rudimentary self images. There is an enormous increase in the intake of information with the development of specialized sensory structures: eyes, ears, and so on. Corresponding to this increased capacity for absorbing information, there is an increased complexity of the image and a greatly increased capacity for learning. It may be, indeed, that this is the most fundamental distinction between the botanical and the zoological world. The image of the plant may be thought of as a property of its genes alone. It is only through mutations of the genes that the plant "learns" anything at all. In the higher organisms, the organism itself learns. Even the fish and the reptile have some sort of image of their environment, and even perhaps, a half-conscious image. They know to some extent where they are in their own limited area and respond to the image rather than to specific stimuli; the more highly developed dogs and apes not only have a degree of self-consciousness, they have quite complex value systems and experience emotions of rage, affection, and so on.

The seventh level of organization is that of the human being. Man is not differentiated from the lower animals by any increased capacity for intake of information. Human eyes and ears are not much better than those of other mammals, and the human nose is almost certainly much worse. It is the capacity for organizing information into large and complex images which is the chief glory of our species. In the area of our image of space we enjoy a much more extended image than do the lower animals. Nevertheless, it is probable that our image is not different in kind. The monkey surely inhabits the same kind of three-dimensional world that we do. Our image of time, however, goes far beyond that of the most intelligent of the lower animals, mainly because of our capacity for language and for record. It is doubtful whether the time image of the lower animals ever goes much beyond the immediate moment, and it is certainly confined to their own private experience. A dog has no idea that there were dogs before him and there will be dogs after him. The human being, on the other hand, is firmly located in a temporal process. He has an image of the past which extends back far beyond the limits of his own life and experience, and he likewise has an image of the future. Closely associated with the time structure of his image is the image of the structure of relationships. Because we are aware of time, we are also aware of cause and effect, of contiguity and succession, of cycles and repetition.

The image of man is also characterized by a much greater degree of self-consciousness and of self-awareness than that of the lower animals. We not only know, but we know that we know. This reflective character of the human image is unique, and is what leads to philosophy. Because of the extended time image and the extended relationship images, man is capable of "rational behavior," that is to say, his response is not to an immediate stimulus but to an image of the future filtered through an elaborate value system. His image contains not only what is, but what might be. It is full of potentialities as yet unrealized. In rational behavior man contemplates the world of potentialities, evaluates them according to his value system, and chooses the "best." Because of his extended image, he is also capable of organizing his own experience in ways that will extend the image further. This is the essence of science and the scientific method. This is in fact a fairly new development in the history of man. It has led, however, to an enormous extension of his image both in time and space and in relationships in the course of the past two hundred years.

Man's image is also characterized by a phenomenal capacity for internal growth and development quite independent of messages received from outside. So great is this capacity, indeed, that it can easily become pathological. In the extreme form we see the schizophrenic who builds up a whole imaginary universe out of the proliferations of his own images without regard to any contradictory messages which may come from outside. It is this property of the "imagination," however, which is also responsible for the greatest achievements of man. Without it our literature, religion, and science would be impossible. Out of the stuff of his image he has built Valhalla and Olympus, symphonies and paintings and poems, fantasies, fairy tales, and novels. Within the image of one man, there exists not only the image of himself but the image of many others. It is this capacity which enables us to enter into complex personal relationships, to build organizations, and to write novels.

Because of his capacity for abstract communication and language and his ability to enter in imagination into the lives of others, man is able to build organizations of a size and complexity far beyond those of the lower animals, even of the social insects. An organization might almost be defined as a structure of roles tied together with lines of communication. The cellular units of organizations are not men, but, as it were, parts of men, men acting in a certain role. Because of this, each man is able to participate in many organizations in different roles and in different parts of his time and activity. There are tempting analogies between the role and the organization, on the one hand, and the cell and the biological organism, on the other, or even between the mitochondria of the cell and the cell itself. All these are open systems in the sense that they maintain a structure in the midst of a through-put of material. The social organization maintains its role structure amid a flow of constantly changing individual persons occupying these roles. Men are continually hired, fired, promoted, and demoted. They join and resign. They are born and they die. The organizations potentially, at least, go on forever. Organizations like organisms exhibit division of labor, specialization of the role, and a hierarchical structure of communication and authority. Just as in the biological organism we must assume some "central agent," to use a term of W. E. Agar, so in the organization, there is an executive or a responsible agent whose decisions are of prime importance in determining the behavior of the organization. The behavior of the organization, however, must be interpreted as a result of the image of the executive, directed by his value system. The executive in the concept of Chester Barnard is strikingly analogous to the control of the thermostatic mechanism. He is a receiver of messages from the receptor of the organization, and his job is to transform these messages into instructions or orders which go out to the effectors. He cannot be regarded, however, as simply a sausage machine grinding out instructions from the messages received. It is much more realistic to suppose that between the incoming and outgoing messages lies the great intervening variable of the image. The outgoing messages are the result of the image, not the result of the incoming messages. The incoming messages only modify the outgoing messages as they succeed in modifying the image.

Part of the image of a man is a more or less public image of the organizations in which he plays a role or which comprise his environment. So far as this public image is a self-conscious one, the organization itself may be said to have self-consciousness. We must beware of analogy here, however. The image is always the property of the individual persons, not of the organization.

Each level of organization includes characteristics from all the lower levels. The clockwork must move some kind of static structure. It has wheels, rods, levers, and so on. The thermostat not only has a static structure, it has some kind of mechanical structure as well. It also must have wheels, wires, currents, air flows, and so on. The cell has a static structure, its anatomy. It has a mechanical structure, in this case mostly chemical. It has a control mechanism maintaining its homeostatic variables. In addition, it is self-maintaining and capable of growth and multiplication. Plants have an anatomy, a dynamics of sap flow and growth. They exhibit a degree of homeostasis, they are open systems and are also capable of organizing cells into a division of labor and structural growth; and they have, in addition, a regular time cycle. Animals have all the above plus a much more elaborate image of the world around them, an image which becomes ever more elaborate as we pass from the fishes through the reptiles to the mammals. Humans have all of the above plus self-consciousness, time-boundness, images of the past, of the future, of causality, of relationship. Perhaps the organizational level alone should be regarded as parallel to the human level rather than above it.

In contemplating the scheme of levels of organization it becomes abundantly clear that at the present stage of human knowledge our theoretical constructs are fairly adequate at the lower levels, but become increasingly inadequate as we proceed to the higher levels. At the level of static structures our theoretical formulations are excellent and almost entirely adequate. We know a great deal about the anatomy of the atom, the molecule, the cell, the organism, and the organization. The weakest link in this chain is perhaps the cell. We do not know very much about the inner anatomy of the cell and still less about the anatomy of the gene or the virus. There is a real gap in our knowledge here, a gap which may also be difficult to close because of the extreme complexity of the structures involved and the even more extreme difficulty of observation. We still do not know how the gene, for instance, which is so small and yet has within it the potentiality of creating all the complexity of the human body, is able to exhibit a structure as intricate as it must have in order to contain this vast potentiality.

The theory of "clockworks" is also well understood. Our technical civilization is built largely upon classical mechanics. It may even increasingly come to be built upon quantum mechanics with the advent of the atomic age. Even at this level there are many gaps in our knowledge, especially in regard to biological structures. Although great advances have been made in this field there is still much in the mechanism of the muscles and the nerves which eludes us. Still less do we understand the mechanics of the brain, which provides the mechanical substratum for the almost infinitely complex images of man. It may well be that a new mechanics will have to be developed in this area just as quantum mechanics had to be developed in the area outside the dimensions of ordinary mechanical experience.

We have begun to understand control mechanisms only in the last few years; nevertheless, the advance has been great, and it may now be claimed that our theoretical models of control mechanisms are about as good as those for mechanics. Perhaps the principal area of ignorance here is a result of our ignorance of the lower mechanical and static structures which underlie the control mechanisms, especially in the case of the gene, the cell, and the embryo. Still less do we have any adequate theory of the homeostatic mechanisms involved in the complex human image. Psychoanalysis has explored some of these. It has not, however, been able to establish any psychophysical base for its theoretical system.

Even at the simplest biological level it is clear that our theoretical structures are quite inadequate. We are beginning to understand something of the machinery of self-maintenance in the theory of open systems. Our ignorance in this field is reflected in our impotence. We have not yet been able to make anything which is capable of self-maintenance, growth, or reproduction. In this sense our cleverest machines, even our great calculating machines fall far behind the skill of the simplest cell. As we move upward in the biological world our ignorance and impotence become even more striking. Medicine is still a medley of science, magic, and inspired guesswork. At the level of human psychology and personality, if we are honest we must admit that we have no adequate models that can explain how people get the way they are. Here again we have important insights, but our image is a mass of confusing messages, not a well-integrated structure.

At the level of society, curiously enough, our theoretical structures seem to be somewhat better than they are at the intermediate levels. Economics, for instance, has a reasonably adequate theoretical system. We have a pretty fair idea of how the price system works, and we know pretty well what are the determinants of the general level of employment and output. Here again, knowledge is reflected in power. We know (I hope) today how to prevent severe depressions. We do not know how to prevent wars, how to eliminate crime, or how to make people happy. We do not even know how to diminish the total amount of mental illness.

With all the gaps in our theoretical structure, one thing is clear. It is that as we proceed from lower to higher levels of organization, the concept of the image becomes an increasingly important part of any theoretical model, and the image itself becomes increasingly complex. At the first and second levels we can get along almost without any concept of the image at all, although there are analogues of the image in the idea of the limitations of static structures and of dynamic processes. The valency of an element in chemistry, for instance, is a concept which has some relationship to the image insofar as it is a kind of "know how." A rudimentary image is exhibited in simple control mechanisms. It is clearly present even at the very earliest stage of life. It grows in importance and complexity as we ascend the biological ladder. It is of overwhelming importance in the interpretation of human behavior and of the dynamics of society.

3

The Image at the Biological Level

I MUST BEGIN THIS CHAPTER with a disclaimer. I am not a biologist and have received no formal training in this area. Indeed, I hardly dare to claim amateur status. What follows, therefore, must be taken as highly tentative. It is a set of suggestions which I hope those competent in the field will sometime feel impelled to develop.

I have already observed that there is something like "knowledge" even at the inorganic level of organization. The atom has a certain kind of "know how" as expressed in its valencies. The carbon atom, for instance, knows how to join with four hydrogen atoms or with two oxygen atoms. It also mysteriously enough knows how to join with one oxygen atom to form carbon monoxide. It is little more than a figure of speech, however, to regard this ability as knowledge. Valency at least in its simpler phases is a fairly well understood mechanical property, and mechanical models on the whole are completely adequate to explain it. The transmutations of radioactive elements in a similar way may be regarded as a kind of "know how," but here again the phenomenon can be dealt with at the level of purely mechanical models.

The basic model of most inorganic systems is the closed

system. This is a system of a given number of variables constrained by some mutual functional relationships which move to some position of minimum potential and remain in this equilibrium. As we move toward the biological sphere, however, the concept of an "open system" becomes of greater and greater importance. An open system we have defined roughly as a structure which maintains itself and develops in the midst of a stream of "through-put." An open system is one which is continually taking in something from its environment and giving out something to its environment, all the while maintaining its structure in the middle of this flow. All organization which comes under the category of life exhibits this characteristic. There are some possible examples of open systems at the molecular level especially as we move toward the colloids, the giant molecules, and the viruses. Within the molecule the subatomic particles may form an open system of some kind, with each atom, as it were, maintaining its structure in the face of a through-put of electrons. In the case even of the simplest living substances, however, there is no doubt that without the concept of an open system their behavior cannot possibly be interpreted.

An important and universal characteristic of the living substance is growth. The growth of living organisms, however, is very different from the growth of inorganic substances like crystals. The growth of living substances is both organized and "equifinal." It is organized in the sense that it involves the orderly differentiation of the substance into complex parts exhibiting a division of labor. By saying that the growth is equifinal we mean that it has some end form, the attainment of which is marked by the cessation of growth and which is strikingly independent of the origin of the system.

We may illustrate the difference between organized and unorganized growth by considering the difference between the growth of a crystal, or even more, of a cancer, and the growth of a well-planned building. Crystals and cancers grow by accretion, a building grows "toward" a blueprint. There is an image in the mind and indeed on the plans of the builder which determines the collection of material and the whole growth of the object. At each stage in the process the builder carefully compares the structure so far achieved with the blueprint, and any divergence is ruthlessly corrected. The growth of living organisms is much more like the growth of a building than it is the growth of a crystal. The genes are both blueprints and carpenters. They are capable of taking the substance of the environment of the growing organism and compelling it to adopt the required forms. The gene, that is to say, must be interpreted as an image.

There is a good deal of evidence for the above point of view from embryology. One of the most striking discoveries of developmental biology is the undifferentiated nature of the early stages of most organisms. Dreisch performed a classical experiment in which he divided the egg of a sea urchin into two parts, each of which grew up into a whole and complete adult. Many experiments have shown that it is not so much the specific character of the part of the egg which determines what it shall grow into but rather the location of the part relative to others. Embryologists distinguish between "regulation" eggs in which the future history of any part is determined not by internal character but by its position in the whole, and "mosaic" eggs in which the history of each part is governed by its internal and specific characteristics. There is considerable evidence that there are in the development of the embryo certain substances known as organizers which,

34

as it were, carry information to the cells to tell them how they shall develop.

What I am arguing here is that in developing any theoretical models of living organization we cannot neglect the through-put not only of the material substance but also of information. Even the simplest living creature is an information-gathering and information-organizing structure. The through-put of information, however, is a very different process from the through-put of material substance. Material substances, in which I include energy, obey strict laws of conservation. The basic law of conservation is that the increase in anything in any system is equal to the difference between what has been taken in and what has been given out. This is true of water in a reservoir, of any element in the body, and it is true also of energy. It is not true, however, of information. The through-put of information in an organization involves a "teaching" or structuring process which does not follow any strict law of conservation even though there may be limitations imposed on it. When a teacher instructs a class, at the end of the hour presumably the students know more and the teacher does not know any less. In this sense the teaching process is utterly unlike the process of exchange which is at the basis of the law of conservation. In exchange, what one gives up another acquires; what one gains another loses. In teaching this is not so. What the student gains the teacher does not lose. Indeed, in the teaching process, as every teacher knows, the teacher gains as well as the student. In this phenomenon we find the key to the mystery of life.

There is a good deal of evidence that just as there is "regulation" within the egg or the embryo so also there is regulation within the chromosomes or general genetic structure itself—that is to say, the "know how" of the individual gene is not dependent merely on its internal structure and specific form. It is dependent also on its place in the over-all structure of the chromosome. However this may be, we must assume that in the case of each organism there is some over-all genetic structure. Genetic structure has two important properties. It is a pattern which is able to impose itself, that is, to reproduce itself on part of the material substance with which it comes into contact. It does this through cell division in which the over-all genetic structure is, as far as we know, simply reproduced. In this sense it acts like a printing machine, printing endless copies of itself on the matter around it. This is what is known as the "genotype."

The genetic structure has, however, an even more astonishing property. It is able to organize the through-put of matter around it not only in a copy of itself but also into an organism wholly unlike itself—the "phenotype" or the biological organism as we see it in nature. Beginning from the one-celled egg the genetic structure organizes this into complex plants, animals, and even human beings. Before the skill of this genetic structure one is lost in admiration. It exceeds in subtlety anything which the human mind has up to now been able to do. Machines of human contrivance, even the most elaborate and beautiful of them, are crude, clumsy, and inept compared with the exquisite machinery of the body which is built by the know-how of the genetic structure. When one reflects that all that we are and do which is not of our own wills was in some sense contained in the fertilized egg that each of us once was, one is inspired to an emotion akin to reverence. The extreme imperfection of our understanding of this process is reflected in our almost complete inability to reproduce it. Nevertheless, we know that it must involve something like an image, that it must involve a "teaching-learning" operation, and that it involves the organization of matter into patterned structures through the transfer of information.

The gene is a wonderful teacher. It is, however, a very poor learner. According to present theories it learns nothing. It changes only by chance variation or mutations, a result perhaps of the accidental impact of radiation or of some chance internal rearrangements of the structure itself. Negative evidence is, of course, always doubtful, and perhaps one should always leave the door slightly ajar for a return to a more Lamarckian interpretation of the changes in the genetic structure—that is, interpreted in modern terms, that the form of the gene may be modified by the experience of the phenotype it creates. It must be admitted, however, that up to the present there is no convincing evidence for this hypothesis. The fact is that we know very little about mutation. We have observed it only over a very short space of time, and we are perhaps all too ready to project through the geological ages conclusions which are derived from a comparatively short length of observation. Let us assume then, at least at the level of first approximation, that the gene learns nothing. It merely teaches and creates new teachers like itself. The genetic structure is the high priest of a rigidly authoritarian culture concerned only with transmitting the truth of its heritage from generation to generation. Changes in the culture come only from outside revelation. They do not arise out of experience. The cultures which have fortunate revelations will survive; those which have unfortunate revelations will not. This gives an appearance of adaptation to the genetic structure. It is, however, purely an appearance and has no basis in reality.

Passing now to the phenotype—the organism which the genetic structure creates—we find a very different picture, even at the simple level of the one-celled organism. The phenotype exhibits phenomena which can only be interpreted on the assumption that the phenotype itself is the possessor of an image of its environment which is not the same as the image of the genetic structure. If the little one-celled animal known as the Paramecium is observed in water, the temperature of which is slowly being raised, it will at first exhibit a somewhat livelier movement simply as a result of the energetics of the system. This livelier movement is in no way different from that exhibited by inorganic substances when their energy is increased. At a certain critical temperature, however, the behavior of the tiny animal changes. Instead of merely speeding up its rather random movements in search of food it now develops what can only be described as "seeking" behavior. The animal swims around in ever-widening circles as if it seeks to escape the hot water in which it finds itself. There is something here like perception. Simple as it is, the Paramecium has an image of the universe around it in which cooler waters may sometimes be found for the seeking.

More remarkable still, the one-celled animal not only has something like an image of its universe, this image can be changed by messages which it receives. In other words, the animal is capable of learning. If we squirt an innocuous dye at a Paramecium it will first exhibit reactions of avoidance. After repeated experience with the substance, however, it learns that it is not harmful and the avoidance reaction ceases. Its image of the universe has been changed by its experience. This change in the image may also be relatively permanent, that is, even the Paramecium has something like memory. The amoeba is capable of recognizing food which it envelops and ingests and in distinguishing this from not-food or

38

from harmful substances which it rejects. There is clearly here an image of the universe divided into food and not-food, and the messages which it receives from the particles with which it comes into contact are interpreted and classified according to this abstract system. Even at this level we see the basic pattern of image formation: messages filtered through a value system.

Certain forms of amoeba are capable of even more astonishing behavior. As long as the food supply is abundant they eat, grow, divide, and so multiply. If, however, food becomes scarce an extraordinary change in their behavior occurs. Thousands of separate cells move together to form a small wormlike object. By means of concerted movements among the cells this object moves forward somewhat on the principle of the inch-worm. After this has moved a certain distance it begins to erect itself into a plantlike object. Differentiation takes place within the separate cells, depending on their position in the object. Those in the stalk become hard and rigid and die. Those in the "flower" eventually transform themselves into a seedlike spore which is then scattered and may remain dormant for a long time until conditions become favorable again. Here is exhibited in most dramatic form the mystery of the plant, that is, the cell society. Can it be doubted that each single-celled amoeba possesses in some sense an image of its function in the social organization and that certain messages that it receives—for instance, the frequency of food ingestion—are interpreted to mean that the drama must now begin?

Communication in the case of the amoeba and probably even the highest plants is conducted entirely by chemical means, as far as we now know. It may be also that the physical substratum of the image in these organisms is likewise of a chemical nature. That is to say, it consists of arrangements of atoms in large and complex molecules. This, of course, is a guess. We have no direct evidence of this point. We can picture, however, the image as a large molecule which is modified by contact with messages in the shape of other molecules presumably smaller and less complex. The limitations of such a system are clear. The possible transformations even of the most complex molecule are extremely limited by the sheer limitations of spatial structure and of chemical valency. The amount of information which is carried by a message is measured by the number of possible arrangements of the carrier. Where the carrier is a chemical compound the amount of information is severely limited because of the fact that the number of compounds is strictly limited.

The next great step in organization which marks the passage from the botanical to the zoological level is the liberation of the organism from purely chemical messages and from a purely chemical communication system. This step represents the addition of electrical or electromagnetic messages to the chemical repertoire. It is not, of course, that chemical messages cease to be important. In the human organism, for instance, the chemical message structure stemming mainly from ductless glands is an extremely important element in the operation of the whole system. Nevertheless, the movement from the purely chemical to the electrical level, which represents in a sense a movement from the strictly atomic level of message bearing to a subatomic level, represents an enormous increase in the possibility of receiving, transmitting, storing, and organizing information. It represents, therefore, a tremendous potential increase in the size and complexity of the image, an increase which to date reaches its highest development in man. The use of electromagnetic messages begins with simple sensitivity to light, which is found at low levels of life and is universal in the plant world. In the internal structure of plants, however, the messages from light waves have to be translated into chemical information before they can be utilized by the plant.

As we pass into the zoological world we find the development of specialized sense receptors, such as eyes and ears, which are able to utilize light waves and sound waves directly and to channel them into the organization through a nervous system using a form of electrochemical communication. Not only do we find the use of electrochemical messages in the receipt of information and in the internal transmission of information through the organism we find also that electrochemical means are used as a physical substratum for the image which the organism possesses. This is the development of the brain. We still know very little about this incredible structure. We know that chemical messages are still employed in it. We know also, however, that the electrochemical or electromagnetic messages proceeding from the nervous system are the most important element, at least in the higher functions. In particular, the development of the cortex represents a tremendous step forward in the amplification of the image. At present it must be confessed that we understand very little about how this image is organized. Indeed, the more we learn about the operations of the brain the more puzzling it becomes. Like the embryo the cortex is remarkably nonspecific in its character. It is true that we can identify certain areas, especially along the Rolandic fissure, which are intimately connected with sensation and movement in different parts of the body. Nevertheless, the brain as a whole seems to be capable of extraordinary powers of transference of function and adaptability. We can remove up to four-fifths of the cortex of a trained rat and the creature will lose remarkably little of what he has learned even though he may take a little time to recover his image. The image clearly does not reside in any one place or location. It is a pattern which pervades the whole.

The contribution which the development of the cortex has made to the image of the organism is illustrated well in this quotation from W. E. Agar: "In the amphibia studied by Weiss the reversed forelimbs continued to the end to function in their original way contrary to the needs of the animal, while in the higher animal muscles which have been artificially connected to a foreign nerve are soon made to function so as to bring about the movements desired by the animal. Weiss attributes this difference between the amphibia and the higher animals to the fact that whereas in both cases the phenomenon of homologous response is due to properties of the spinal motor centers, in the higher animals there is greater cerebral control of the centers."[1] The unfortunate salamander which does not enjoy the luxury of a developed cortex finds that if its limbs are reversed it is quite incapable of going anywhere and it is never able to correct this situation. This means in all probability that its image does not include a self-image. It is aware of some sort of universe around it. It interprets the messages which come to its sense organs, as for instance, food out there toward which it will run or danger out there away from which it will run. It does not, however, see its legs as performing those running functions. The higher mammal on the other hand is capable of retraining its lower nervous center to conform to the image which it has of itself.

A further interesting example of the function of the

1. W. E. Agar, *A Contribution to the Theory of the Living Organism* (2nd ed.; Melbourne, 1951), p. 95.

cortex in elaborating the image is to be found in the behavior of the decorticated dog. If meat which has been spiked with quinine to make it bitter-tasting is presented to a hungry normal dog, the dog after some initial hesitation will eventually eat the meat. A decorticated dog on the other hand no matter how hungry or even starving it may be will not eat ill-tasting meat. Its image of the universe is limited to the differentiation between good-tasting food and bad-tasting food. It is not capable of extending itself to the concept of food in general. The normal dog clearly has this concept and is able to overcome the repugnance of the lower centers because it has a hierarchy of images in the cortex. The contrast between the reflex-operated action of the lower nervous centers and the image-operated action of the higher centers could hardly be better illustrated. One and the same message produces a totally different response in the two cases. It is rejected on a simple stimulus-response basis by the lower centers. It is accepted by the higher centers because it is interpreted into an image. The behavior is response to an image, not a response to a stimulus, and without the concept of an image the behavior cannot possibly be understood. The dog is oriented in space: he can find his way home even from a place where he has never been before. He is oriented in a world of relationships, food as distinguished from not-food, in spite of superficial appearances. He is oriented in a world of personality. He recognizes certain messages as meaning master or mistress and other messages as meaning enemy. What the dog cannot do and what no lower animal can do is talk. It is this capacity for language which is the most essential difference between man and all other organisms.

From the point of view of their effect on the image the messages which constitute the stream of incoming information to an organism may be classified into signs and symbols. A sign is a message which alters the image of the immediate universe around the organism. In Pavlov's experiments, dogs were "conditioned" to salivate at the sound of the bell by always presenting food to them when the bell rang. What this means is that the bell produced a change in the image exactly corresponding to the change in the image which the sight and the smell induced. The bell was the sign of food just as, however, the scent and the sight was a sign of food. What one cannot do to a dog is to make him salivate by telling him a story about food. This is something which can be done to a human. A symbol, therefore, may have no effect and indeed ordinarily will have no effect on the image of the immediate universe around one. It does produce an effect, however, of what might be called the image of the image, on the image of the future, on the image of the past, on the image of the potential or even the image of the impossible. It is this ability to proliferate and elaborate the image into a symbolic universe that is the peculiarity and the glory of man. When I hear someone speaking to me the noise of his words is a sign. It changes or confirms my image of his presence in the room with me. The sign would be just as good if he were talking nonsense or if he were talking an unintelligible tongue as if he were talking sense in a language which I understand. If, however, he is talking in a language I understand there are symbolic changes in my image, changes which refer not to the immediate universe around me but to the whole content of my imagination. It is this symbolic image and the communications which establish it and which change it which constitutes the peculiar quality of human society, a quality which no animal society shares. In the lowest society, whether of the social insects or of cells, there is communication. The communication, however, is in signs, not in symbols. That is to say, the effect of the message on the image is to change the image of the world around, not to create an image of nonexistent worlds.

The biological basis of the symbolic powers of man is very obscure. There are, indeed, certain biological prerequisites in the form of elaborate speech systems and cortical centers which are necessary before a symbolic system can be developed. It is a puzzling problem in the evolution of man to know how these elaborate speech and auditory centers could possibly have developed in the absence of symbolic structure in the image, for without the symbolic structure they could have no function. On the other hand, it is also difficult to see how the symbolic structure could possibly have developed without the elaborate speech and hearing apparatus. The lack of speech in the apes and the lower animals seems to be a result both of an absence of symbolic representation and also an absence of elaborate speech and hearing centers. Nevertheless, however we got this way, here we are. The study of man is the study of talk. Human society is an edifice spun out of the tenuous webs of conversation.

One final question of great interest which must also go unanswered is the relationship of the symbolic image to consciousness, especially to self-consciousness. The lower animals have awareness. The image of dogs and monkeys, for instance, probably includes some differentiation between sleeping and waking conditions. It may be doubted whether any animal apart from man has what could properly be called self-consciousness, that is, an image of its image. Consciousness, however, is a baffling and impenetrable mystery. The most that we can say about it is that it is intimately connected with the symbolic process and that it is profoundly affected by disturbances of the symbolic process. We cannot even conceive of ourselves, however, as building a machine or a construction with consciousness. It is easy to build stimulus-response machines. It is even possible to build, as W. R. Ashby has done, something like a learning machine, a machine that is capable of conditioned reflexes. We can build machines to do elaborate calculations or even to play chess. We can build machines with memory, that is, with stored information. We have not succeeded in building the simplest machine with a conscious image. When we do that we will, in a very real sense, have created a new form of intelligence.

The Image of Man and Society

THE IMAGE OF MAN
is rich and complex beyond expression. It is a curious
paradox that although this very richness is a result of its
symbolic character, symbols and language are incapable
of expressing it to the full. There is always something
in the image of man, even of the most intelligent and
sophisticated person "beyond what words can utter."
Nevertheless, it is possible to abstract from this richness
and to discuss the human image in terms of a relatively
few important dimensions. I have already given a brief
outline of these in Chapter I. We may classify these aspects of the image in the following way; this classifica-
tion is tentative but it may be helpful. We have first the
spatial image, the picture of the individual's location in
the space around him. We have next the temporal image,
his picture of the stream of time and his place in it.
Third, we have the relational image, the picture of the
universe around him as a system of regularities. Perhaps
as a part of this we have, fourth, the personal image, the
picture of the individual in the midst of the universe of
persons, roles, and organizations around him. Fifth, we
have the value image which consists of the ordering on
the scale of better or worse of the various parts of the

whole image. Sixth, we have the affectional image, or emotional image, by which various items in the rest of the image are imbued with feeling or affect. Seventh, we have the division of the image into conscious, unconscious, and subconscious areas. Eighth, we have a dimension of certainty or uncertainty, clarity or vagueness. Ninth, we have a dimension of reality or unreality, that is, an image of the correspondence of the image itself with some "outside" reality. Tenth, closely related to this but not identical with it, we have a public, private scale according to whether the image is shared by others or is peculiar to the individual.

The spatial image can exhibit varying degrees of sophistication. This may have a profound effect on other parts of the image. All human beings, without exception, seem to inhabit a three-dimensional world, an image which is certainly shared by most higher animals. In his least sophisticated spatial image man probably pictures himself as occupying the approximate center of a flat plane with the sky above and the earth below. Only within the last few hundred years has there come general acceptance of the more sophisticated view of the earth as a ball suspended in almost empty space, rotating around a sun which is a star, a member of a galaxy of stars, which in turn is a member of a universe of galaxies. This change in spatial orientation from the old three-story universe, even of the Middle Ages, to the sophisticated universe of today, is a profound one, and has had a marked effect on man's image of himself in many aspects. It has, perhaps, deflated his self-importance, but it has led to serious problems in his image of his prevailing religions, most of which are phrased in terms of an unsophisticated cosmology.

All human beings, except perhaps the extremely mentally deranged, regard themselves as oriented in some way in a stream of time. There are some interesting questions regarding the different ways in which different cultures, as evidenced by their languages, have oriented themselves in this time stream, but these we will have to leave with a brief mention. The picture which is common to Western civilization of a one-dimensional time stream flowing at a constant rate with a point, the present, dividing the past from the future, is by no means universal. In many primitive cultures, the time concept is more circular than linear. There is a time to do this and a time to do that, and this process repeats itself endlessly. In a very real sense, such a culture has no history. All summers are the same summer; all deaths are the same death; all births are the same birth. With the coming of history, however, and the closely associated written records, the tendency for the time concept to become linear and for history to be viewed as a one-way street, is almost universal. The more sophisticated concepts of space and time implied in the theory of relativity have not yet had much effect on popular images. There is a curious dilemma here. As science becomes more and more sophisticated, it becomes further divorced from the popular images and less capable of influencing them.

The relational dimension of the image consists in the supposed stabilities which may be put in the form of hypothetical sentences: if A, then B. The relational image varies greatly from culture to culture, and even within subcultures within the same general society. The stability of the relational image is one of the most interesting questions, not only for anthropologists and other students of culture, but for the philosophers of science. The relational images of primitive people contain many relationships which disappear in the course of sophistication.

There are relationships, for instance, between ceremonial acts and the natural world. The belief in witchcraft and magic is all part of the unsophisticated relational image. Even in sophisticated societies, however, the relational image varies greatly from person to person, especially in the area of personal relationships. One of the universal problems here is, when is a message to be interpreted as having relational significance, and when is it to be interpreted as a chance or random event. This is a problem of no mean importance, even in science. Science, of course, represents the most sophisticated attempt to deal with the relational image. Even here, however, relational images arise through strong filtering of messages through the value structure of the scientific subculture. There are many areas of experience which are not respectable for scientists to study and which they investigate with grave risks to their reputations. An important aspect of the relational image is the image of the relation between the acts of the individual and their effects. We may regard this part of the relational image as consisting of a number of potential futures or time images, each of which is associated with some particular mode of behavior in the present. The image can be expressed in a series of sentences: if I do A, then B, C, D, etc., will follow in a definite time succession.

The value image is enormously important in its effects, but remarkably obscure in its origins. Incoming messages are not admitted to the image free. At the gate of the image stands the value system demanding payment. This is as true of sensory messages as it is of symbolic messages. We now know that what used to be regarded as primary sense data are in fact highly learned interpretations. We see the world the way we see it because it pays us and has paid us to see it that way. The value system is quite fundamental in motivation theory. We must think of the image of the individual as including a value ordering of potential acts and their consequences. The act which stands highest on the ordering will be the one performed, and as soon as it is performed, a new ordering comes into view, and a new act is selected. The study of the value image is made difficult by the fact that only a small part of it is usually accessible to the immediate consciousness; consequently, it is common to find that what looks like a change in the value image is actually a change in the position of the individual in the field of the image in general. Poor people and poor societies, for instance, are apt to seem highly materialistic. They lay great stress on the acquisition of material things. Rich societies and rich individuals are apt not to be concerned for material things, but to emphasize the "more spiritual" aspects of life. This difference may be much more the result of a difference of the position of the individual in the field rather than a difference in the value ordering itself. We all tend to value highly what is scarce in our own particular part of the field. The obsession of the poor, both individuals and societies, with material things, may be merely a reflection of their scarcity and not a reflection of a basic difference in value orientation. In a similar way, the sick make a religion of health; the violent make a religion of love; and the self-centered make a religion of objectivity.

The affectional image is closely related to the value image but is not necessarily identical with it. The image of the universe as we view it is colored deeply with affects and emotions. We like one thing; we dislike another. We hate one thing; we love another. We are indifferent to A; we fear B; we are overjoyed about C. It is not these affections and emotions, however, which govern our behavior but the value images which we place upon them.

We cannot simply classify the emotions as good or bad, desirable or undesirable, as moving us toward or away from the object which inspires them. Man is deeply ambivalent between his affections and his values, and what is more, he values this ambivalence. Fear, pain, and even death itself have been highly valued by certain individuals and societies. There is almost infinite variation in the value systems which people have placed on the affections and emotions.

Modifying all of the above, we might indicate two more possible dimensions of the image: the certainty-uncertainty dimension, and the reality-unreality dimension. Some things we are sure about; some things we are unsure about; and every aspect of the image (including the value and affectional image) is tinged with some degree of certainty or uncertainty. This is particularly true of the relational image. Closely related to this dimension but not perhaps identical with it is the dimension of reality and unreality. We are very sure that the house we live in, the furniture and utensils that we use, and the people that we know around us, are "real" in the sense that they are not products of our imagination, that they would continue to exist "outside" us, even if we disappeared from the scene. Similarly, dreams, imaginings, fairy stories, legends are perceived as unreal, as not having any existence outside of the human image. The reality-unreality dimension is quite independent of the philosophical question as to whether in fact there is a real world outside our perceptions. Reality or unreality here is a property of the image itself. We can afford to beg the whole philosophical question of idealism versus realism.

Finally, we have an important dimension of consciousness, unconsciousness, and subconsciousness. As part of the image there is something analogous to a scanning mechanism: we are not conscious of all parts of the image at once with the same degree of intensity. This is true even in the field of perception; for instance, in vision, we see only a very small part of our field of vision with anything like accuracy of detail. By scanning, however, we are able to obtain a clear mental image of the whole visual universe around us. Similarly, a very small part of our image is exposed to our internal view at any one time. On the other hand, we have the property of recall. This is a rather mysterious operation. How do we know what to recall before we have recalled it? Nevertheless, there is clearly some process at work whereby those parts of the image which lie in the unconscious can be brought into conscious view. We have a curious capacity for giving ourselves examinations. We know how to write the questions that we have answers for.

Freud has made it clear that in addition to the conscious and unconscious parts of the image, there is also a vast area of the subconscious. This may be defined as that part of the unconscious image which is not available by the scanning process and which cannot be brought into conscious view by any simple act of will. The mind of man is a vast storehouse of forgotten memories and experiences. It is much more than a storehouse, however. It is a genuine image affecting our conduct and behavior in ways that we do not understand with our conscious mind. It is one of the main objects of psychotherapy to bring the subconscious into consciousness or at least into the unconscious where it can be recalled at will. Only when our whole image, as it were, is capable of being spread before us, can we organize it as a unit. Extreme cases are known in which a single biological individual contains two images, two personalities which may alternate with each other.

The recognition of the existence of the subconscious image enables us perhaps to integrate the rational with the irrational. We can now see all behavior as governed by the image and its value system. Rational behavior is that which is governed by the part of the image which is accessible to consciousness. What is usually called irrational behavior, in fact, follows the same principles. It still consists in contemplating a set of future alternatives and the corresponding acts and selecting the highest of these on our value scales. In the case of so-called irrational behavior, however, both the expected consequences and the value scales may be hidden in the subconscious.

We turn now to the consideration of the place of the image in the dynamics of society. We must emphasize from the first that the image is a property of the individual person. It is only by way of metaphor and analogy that we can speak of organizations or of society as a whole as possessing an image. Nevertheless, there are images of some individuals in society, and parts of the image of most individuals which can properly be regarded as an image of the society itself even though the image is "in the minds of the individuals."

In thinking about the relation of images to society, therefore, we must first think of the inventory of the images of the individuals who compose the society. This may be thought of in the first instance as a simple list of the images of individuals a, b, c, etc. We next consider the dynamic processes by which these individual images are maintained and changed.

The stock of images in a society is changed in the first instance by all those things which change individual images, that is, by learning processes. If we want to study, therefore, the dynamics of the image stock of a society, we must first study the way in which messages change the images of the individuals in the society. The messages which impinge on the individual image come partly from "nature" and partly from other persons or other instruments in the society. In considering the dynamics of the stock of images the rise of writing and literary communication is of enormous importance. In a nonliterate society messages come from only two sources: from nature, that is from nonhuman sources, or from face-to-face contact with other persons, in speech or nonverbal communication. The invention of writing marks the separation of the communication from the communicator and enables individuals to receive messages from people that they have never met, will never meet, and could never meet. With the invention of writing, messages from individuals may penetrate the time space of the society far beyond the life span of the individuals concerned. In some degree, of course, this is possible in a nonliterate society through the transmission of an oral heritage. Writing, however, enormously magnifies this effect. In our own day we have seen the still further extension of the principle of the separation of the communication from the communicator through the development of mass media. Printing enables one communicator to communicate with millions of other individuals. The invention of the radio, the phonograph, the movie, television has still further separated the communicator from the communication. What this means is that all of the signals which proceed from any individual can now be disseminated literally to all others present and to come. We have established one-way, face-to-face contact through the mass media, between the communicator and millions of other persons. Through television, for instance, an individual may be almost literally present in all the living rooms of the nation.

It is important, however, to notice that with all the developments of mass communication such communication is still "one way." In two-way communication there is still no substitute for face-to-face contact. Even letters and telephones are poor substitutes for the living presence. We shall develop this point further in the next chapter.

The stock of images in society is changed not only through the communication processes of the society. It is changed also by the turnover of individuals through birth and death and the succession of the generations. A society does not consist of a fixed stock of individuals. Individuals are added to the stock all the time through birth, through growth and maturation; and they are subtracted all the time through death. If we confined our view of the dynamics of the stock of images, therefore, solely to the processes by which the image changes in the individual, we would be seriously misled. In discussing the dynamics of the image in society, therefore, we must lay considerable stress on the problem of the relationships among the generations. The basic structure of the individual image is mainly laid down in early childhood and there is much to be said for the stress which has been placed in recent years on the close relationship between practices in the rearing of children and the personality types of a society.

This view can, of course, be carried too far. It is too much to attribute the whole personality of a society to its practices in the toilet training of children. The image continues to grow and develop long after childhood and, indeed, there is much to be said for the point of view that the years of adolescence are at least as critical in determining the major parts of the image as are the years of early childhood. In many important aspects, also, the image continues to grow and to change throughout life. Nevertheless, the relationships among the generations are of great importance in establishing the dynamics in a stock of images and in explaining the subtle shift in the "flavor" of a society from generation to generation.

A society consists not only of individual persons; it consists of organizations. Individuals are grouped into many "Leviathans" both large and small: states, churches, businesses, families, trade unions, universities, and so on. We have already defined an organization as a structure of roles tied together by lines of communication. The existence of such a structure depends on the presence of a "public image" among those who participate in its roles. This does not mean, of course, that every individual participating in any organization must have an identical image of the organization itself. The image of a great corporation which is possessed by the president of the company is very different from the image of the same corporation possessed by the janitor. Indeed, it is usually essential to the operation of an organization that there should not be the same image of the organization in the minds of the various participants. It is the image of the role which is significant, not the image of the whole organization. But the images of the roles must be consistent with the over-all image of the organization itself.

The power of organizations to survive in a society depends largely upon the nature of the stock of images of that society. The General Motors Corporation, for instance, would be quite inconceivable in ancient Rome because the Romans did not possess the requisite set of images. It is true also, of course, that organizations require a certain material environment for their continued survival or existence. General Motors, for instance, could not exist in our society, even with all our images as they are, if there were no iron ore or no rubber, and no substitutes for these things. Nevertheless, the artifacts, that is, the physical capital of a society must be regarded as the result of the structuring of the material substance by an image. There is a close analogy here between the image and the gene. The production of an automobile is a process whereby certain parts of the material structure of the earth are arranged into the form of a previous image. The genetics of the automobile is, of course, much more complicated than that of the horse. It is multisexual and, unlike the gene, the image does not merely exhibit random mutation but has a regular systematic and accumulative mode of change. Nevertheless, it is by no means fanciful to argue that the automobile and other human artifacts are produced as a result of a genetic process in which an image plays somewhat the same role as the gene does in the biological world.

It is instructive to consider both the similarities and the differences between social organizations and organisms in the biological world. Like the organism, the organization is an "open system" in the sense that it has a through-put of individuals occupying various places in a role structure much as a biological organism maintains a through-put of material substance in a constant structure. The organization, therefore, exhibits many characteristics of open systems. It has a kind of embryology, and it exhibits a certain degree of equifinality. The organization begins, shall we say, as a fertile image in the mind of some creative individual. Because of his powers of communication this individual is able to implant this image or at least appropriate modifications of this image in the minds of others. Insofar as the image involves the idea of a division of labor, as the organization grows, the division of labor itself begins and the various participating individuals begin to assume different roles. Just as in the development of the embryo, it is frequently the position in the structure which determines the future history of the part, so in the development of the organization, the role which is assigned to an individual often by chance determines his own development. As an organization grows certain significant changes in structure may have to take place. Large organizations must have a different structure from small organizations. In the growth of the business firm, for instance, there seems to be a critical stage below which simple face-to-face communication is feasible, above which it is not, and elaborate organizational structures have to be set up. The change from the informal to the hierarchical organization is not wholly dissimilar to the change from the single-celled organism to the multi-cellular organism. In the organization, as in the organism, the complexity seems to be purchased at the price of mortality. We do not understand very well the processes of decay and death of organization, either in the biological or the organizational world. In both worlds, however, these processes can clearly be observed even though we do not understand them well enough to know whether they are absolutely necessary.

We must be careful, however, against being carried away by analogy. There are extremely important differences between organizations and organisms. The great difference lies in the nature of the image possessed by the constituent parts and by the whole. In the case of the organism, we must regard the image held by the central agent or the organism as a whole as greatly superior in complexity and in content to the image of any of its component parts. We have already seen that it is not illegitimate to regard the individual cell as having an image of some kind. The image of the whole organism, however, is much more elaborate and complete than that of any individual cell. In the case of organizations, the reverse is true. It is the cell which has the image, not the organization. The image structure lies wholly within the frames of the individuals composing the organizations. It does not lie in the relationships of these individuals.

The correct analogy to the image of the organization in the organism is what might be called the genetic image. As far as the genetics of organisms is concerned, it is the image of the cell that is important, not the image of the organization as a whole. Because of this fact, an organization, although it is an open system, is an open system of a very different and much more complex character than that of the biological organism. It is true, of course, that the image of the role to some extent imposes itself on the individual occupying the role. When a man becomes the President of the United States, he begins to behave like a President of the United States, whatever his previous character and behavior. The individual, however, never merely passively fits a role. He reorganizes the role itself through the operation of his own peculiar images. When a square peg is fitted into a round role it is true that the peg becomes rounder, but it is also true that the role becomes squarer. In the dynamics of society, therefore, this constant interaction between the role and the personality is a dominating characteristic.

In spite of the fact that an organization does not properly have an image of its own, curiously enough there is something analogous to the phenomenon of self-consciousness in the field of organization. This self-consciousness is the property of the public image of the organization which is shared by those who participate in it or are related to it. There is a profound difference, for

60

instance, in the image of organizations which is held in primitive and sophisticated societies. Primitive man is, of course, aware of the organizations in which he participates. He is aware, for instance, that he is a member of the tribe. The picture of his society, however, is an unself-conscious one. He accepts the representation of the society as it is handed down to him by his elders in an unquestioning and unself-conscious spirit. A visiting anthropologist, on the other hand, has a self-conscious image of the same society and even of his own society.

This rise in the self-consciousness of the image of society and organization is of great importance in interpreting the dynamics of social change and of the change in the social image. It is unquestionably the main element in the enormous increase in the speed of change and in the rate of mutation of the social image which has taken place in the last few thousand years. It is bound up, of course, with the increase in the image of the time span of the individual and his society which comes through the invention of historic records. It comes even more through the increase in the complexity of the image of relationship with the rise of science and of the social sciences. An extremely interesting example of the rise of self-consciousness of the social image is the development of nationalism, especially democratic nationalism in the last few hundred years. There is a great contrast, for instance, between the image of society as it existed in medieval Europe and as it exists today. This rise in national consciousness has not, of course, been an unmixed blessing, although it has important positive elements. The continued rise of self-consciousness of the image of society is as corrosive to nationalism, however, as it was of prenational images. The social image goes through three stages to disintegration. In the first stage, we find that people believe in it. This is the unself-conscious stage. People think of themselves, for instance, as Americans, or as British, or as Germans, without ever questioning the notion. In the second stage, people believe in believing in it. They see the world as divided into nations. They see, however, that they might just as well have been something else from what they are. Once the image has reached this stage it is a short step to not believing in it at all. The same history is repeated in many religions.

Another very interesting example of the importance of the idea of self-consciousness in the social image is to be found in Marxist theory. This time it is a class consciousness rather than a national consciousness which is regarded as the important part of the image. Marx himself regarded his principal contribution as the giving of class consciousness to the previously unconscious proletariat. He regarded the function of the intellectual in the historic process as the task of making manifest what is latent. The latent, however, cannot be made manifest without transforming it, and the acid of self-consciousness is even more powerful in attacking the idea of class than it is in attacking the idea of the nation.

In the idea of the self-consciousness of the image of the organization, there is something akin to the notion of a "central agent" in the biological organism. An analogy, however, must be taken with extreme caution for reasons which have been outlined above. The organization, like the organism, has a phenotype and a genotype. A university, for instance, has a phenotype in the form of a campus, buildings, ceremonial, a schedule, a calendar, a program. Professors and students come and go, but the university goes on, almost forever. Nevertheless, in the case of organization, the image resides in the genotype, not in the phenotype. Because of the hierarchical structure, there may be some individuals whose images are of peculiar importance in an organization. The phenotype of a university moves more toward the image of the president than it does toward the image of the humble instructor. Nevertheless, in the dynamics of an organization all images are important and none can be neglected. We must always operate with the concept of an inventory of images and we can never replace this inventory by a single image, not even that of the most important person in the organization.

The Public Image
and the Sociology of Knowledge

THE IMAGE NOT ONLY MAKES SOCIETY, society continually remakes the image. This hen and egg process is perhaps the most important key to the understanding of the dynamics of society. The basic bond of any society, culture, subculture, or organization is a "public image," that is, an image the essential characteristics of which are shared by the individuals participating in the group. It is with the dynamics of the public image that we shall chiefly be concerned in this chapter. We must not suppose, of course, that society has no influence on private, unshared images or that these unshared images have no influence on society. Indeed, every public image begins in the mind of some single individual and only becomes public as it is transmitted and shared. Nevertheless, an enormous part of the activity of each society is concerned with the transmission and protection of its public image; that set of images regarding space, time, relation, evaluation, etc., which is shared by the mass of its people.

A public image almost invariably produces a "transcript"; that is, a record in more or less permanent form which can be handed down from generation to generation. In primitive nonliterate societies the transcript takes the form of verbal rituals, legends, poems, ceremonials, and the like, the transmission of which from generation to generation is always one of the principal activities of the group. The invention of writing marks the beginning of the "disassociated transcript"—a transcript which is in some sense independent of the transcriber, a communication independent of the communicator. As we have already noticed, the transcript of society has been in process of rapid development and elaboration in the past few centuries. Beginning with the inventing of printing, and especially with the coming of the camera, the movie, the phonograph, and the tape recorder the elaboration of the transcript has proceeded to the point where an enormous number of aspects of life and experience can be recorded directly. There are still large parts of the image, however, which can only be transcribed in symbolic form. Generations yet unborn may be able to see President Eisenhower in three-D as he appeared to the present-day observer. They will be able to hear the exact cadences of his voice as well as read the words he has written. We are still, however, unable to record touch, taste, or smell. We have no direct means of transcribing sensations, emotions, or feelings except through the crowded channels of symbolic representation.

An effective transcript has a great effect in creating a public image, that is, in ensuring that the images of the various individuals who have access to the transcript are identical or nearly so. As an example of the building-up of a public image through the development of a transcript we might consider the formation of maps. The spatial image can be transcribed very briefly and commodiously in the form of a map. The map itself, however, has a profound effect on our spatial image. When we look at the crudely constructed charts of the South Sea

Islanders they mean very little to us because we visualize the sea as a plain blue surface dotted with multicolored dots which we interpret as islands. The South Sea Islanders probably visualize their space in a somewhat different way in terms of the things you have to do to get from one place to another, the stars you have to observe, the directions you have to go, the courses you have to keep. Instead of being a plain blue surface their space is a series of intersecting lines. The Romans had only vague ideas of the shape of their own empire. They knew pretty well, however, how far it was from Rome wherever they happened to be, and their maps indicate this spatial conception. The maps of the Middle Ages show the world centering in Jerusalem. The shapes were unimportant. The theological symbolism was the vital thing. With the coming of surveying, trigonometry, and accurate measurements the map becomes an exact representative of the bird's-eye view. The invention of latitude and longitude reduced the multidirectional space of earlier days to two simple directions, north-south, east-west. The gradual exploration of the globe leads to a closure of geography. This has profound effects upon all parts of the image. Primitive man lives in a world which has a spatial unknown, a dread frontier populated by the heated imagination. For modern man the world is a closed and completely explored surface. This is a radical change in spatial viewpoint. It produces effects in all other spheres of life.

We learn our geography mostly in school, not through our own personal experience. I have never been to Australia. In my image of the world, however, it exists with 100 per cent certainty. If I sailed to the place where the map makers tell me it is and found nothing there but ocean I would be the most surprised man in the world. I hold to this part of my image with certainty, however, purely on authority. I have been to many other places which I have found on the map and I have almost always found them there. It is interesting to inquire what gives the map this extraordinary authority, an authority greater than that of the sacred books of all religions. It is not an authority which is derived from any political power or from any charismatic experience. As far as I know it is not a crime against the state nor against religion to show a map that has mistakes in it. There is, however, a process of feedback from the users of maps to the map maker. A map maker who puts out an inaccurate map will soon have this fact called to his attention by people who use the map and who find that it violates their spatial image derived from personal experience. The map maker usually places a high value on accuracy, that is, upon not receiving any such adverse criticism. This high valuation upon accuracy may be derived from purely internal standards of workmanship. A map maker who is caught out in an error suffers from internal devaluation of his own skill and therefore of his own person. There may also, of course, be external sanctions. The map maker who puts out inaccurate maps will find it hard to sell them, at least if he makes claims for accuracy. A few years ago a department of the United States government put out a map of the United States in which through the inadvertency of the draftsman a considerable portion of what is officially Texas was assigned to Mexico. The map had hardly been published before the indignation of Texans reached such a volume that it was hastily withdrawn from circulation.

Even the map, which is apparently the most "factual" of all transcripts, may have strong elements involving other parts of the image. This is particularly true of political maps which one sometimes thinks are one of the principal sources of international conflict. A serious international situation was caused in Central America not long ago when one of the countries issued a stamp showing a map which represented its territorial ambitions rather than its territorial realities. It has been seriously suggested that the history of World War I was profoundly affected by the fact that in school atlases of the old German Empire the United States and Germany each occupied a single page. This led to a serious underestimate on the part of the Germans of the size and capacity of the United States.

The public image of time is enormously affected by the nature of the transcript of the society. In primitive societies where the transcript consists mainly in oral tradition, the transmission of which is difficult, there is great fear of a change in the transcript. The emphasis is upon the transmission of the heritage from one generation to another, unspoiled, unsullied, and unaltered by the events of the day. The time image of nonliterate societies therefore has a strong tendency to be circular in character. Its basic notion is not that of succession but that of appropriateness, of the "right" time to do this or that. With the written transcript comes history and the learning of history in formal education. This is again a factor of great importance in determining the whole image of the individual. One of the main purposes of national education is to distort the image of time and space in the interests of the nation. The school atlases have one's own nation large and others small. The school history books have the history of one's own nation large and of others small. It is the history teachers above all who create the image of the Englishman, the German, the American, or the Japanese. This also is an important source of war.

The writers of history also have a license which the map makers do not have. Map makers are continually checked by the fact that it is possible to travel through space. Historians are free from this particular form of feedback because of the fact that we cannot travel through time. An error in a history book, therefore, cannot be rectified by personal experience. We cannot go back to Henry VIII and ask him if he really had six wives in the way that we can go to Australia and see with our own eyes that there is a continent where the map makers say there is. The records of time can only be checked against other records of time, and many of these records are irretrievably lost. The task of the historian is always to make bricks without straw, to make what he believes are correct images of the past from an extremely imperfect sample of recorded data. It is no wonder that history is so phenomenally subject to abuse, that it becomes the agent of propaganda, and also that it is so continually being rewritten.

One of the most interesting things about history is the history of history, that is, the way in which the discovery of new records and the reinterpretation of old ones continually modifies the image of the past. Two examples may be noted. The discovery of the documents of Greece and Rome, or perhaps one should say their rediscovery, for the West at the time of the Renaissance had a profound effect not only on the view of history but also on the whole image, temper, and spirit of the age. In a very real sense the classical past was relived in the Renaissance. Another example is the effect of the discovery of the Egyptian papyri on the interpretation of the New Testament.

The relational image also is largely transmitted by the transcript. In primitive societies and to some extent in all societies, this takes the form of proverbs and wise sayings handed down from parent to child and even more from grandparent to grandchild. Part of the relational image, of course, comes through direct experience. It is not quite so inaccessible as the image of the past. The burnt child receives a vigorous message from nature regarding the relationship between heat and pain. The unburnt child, however, likewise dreads the fire because it has been taught to do so by its elders who speak with the voice of authority. Probably by far the larger portion of our relational image comes with the authority of the transcript not with the authority of experience. For this reason it is possible for the relational image to exhibit wild and fantastic growth especially in primitive cultures where the complexity of the relational image prevents it from being directly verified by experience. The value system which places high value upon messages which conform to the tradition, that is, to the transcript, operates to select those messages which conform to the transcript and to reject those which contradict it. From these forces superstition is born. Particularly where the relational image gives as causes acts and duties on the part of the individual that are all too easily neglected it is constantly confirmed by messages. The relational image that those whose heart is pure will have the strength of ten is constantly being verified by the plainly observable relation that the weak are no Galahads. If it is believed that the crops will not grow unless magical ceremonies are performed every failure of the crops will be met by a rewarding searching of the heart, for on reflection something will be found to be wrong with every ceremony.

It is the peculiar glory of science that it has systematized the growth of the relational image within its subculture in a way that enables it to tread lightly over the relational quicksands of common sense. Where connections are constant and functions are stable science can find them. By measurement, careful observation, controlled experiment, and statistical methods science explores the relational world with much the same kind of feedbacks that guide the map maker. The scientist who proclaims a relation is in much the same position as the map maker who issues a map. He is in danger of being put to shame by anyone who cannot find the relation that he has announced. Science, however, buys its success at a price; indeed at a high price. The price is a severe limitation of its field of inquiry and a value system which is as ruthless in its own way in the censoring of messages as the value system of primitive man. Messages which will not conform to the subculture are condemned as illusion. Furthermore, the world of the scientist is the world of the repeatable, the world of the probable. The rare occurrence, the nonrepeatable event, the unanswerable question elude him.

That part of the relational image which deals with the relations among persons is peculiarly subject to strange dynamic instability arising out of the fact that persons themselves are to a considerable extent what their images make them. Because the image is a creation of the message people tend to remake themselves in the image which other people have of them. Personal relations, therefore, involve an extremely complex action and reaction of image upon image. If I think that Mr. A is a mean and surly individual I will treat him in such a way that he will become meaner and more surly. If I think he is a good fellow I will treat him in such a way as to increase his affability. So there is opportunity here for fantastic dynamic series of misinterpretation, misunderstanding, frustrations, and breakdowns. We must reckon with the fact that in passing from one person to another messages become strangely transformed. My friend lets fall an innocent remark which I interpret falsely as being hostile and before we know where we are my action and his reaction and my reaction have made us enemies. We are dealing here with a world of mirrors and it is often hard to see what is being reflected.

The impact of society on the image is nowhere more apparent or more important than in the value image. We may suppose, of course, that there is a basic "biological" value image which is built into the organism by its genetic constitution. The process of natural selection alone would justify some such assumption. An organism which put a high value on pain, hunger, and self-immolation would be somewhat unlikely to survive in the course of the evolutionary process. The modern psychologist assumes that these biological values exist in the form of certain elementary drives, hunger, thirst, pain, fear, and sex. The specific forms which these drives take, however, are elaborated and varied almost beyond belief by the baroque processes of acculturation. Indeed, what might be called the acquired values in many cases dominate the biological ones. Because of their hunger and thirst after righteousness men willingly endure the hunger and thirst of the body, chastity, pain, torment, and even death itself. Survival is not the highest human value. One doubts, indeed, whether it is even the highest value in the biological world. One suspects that survival is frequently a byproduct of the play of genetic forces. It is by the willingness to risk death that both men and animals gain life.

For most people there can be little doubt that the value image is mainly a product of a transcript. Education in most societies is a matter of harnessing the biological drives in the interests of establishing the value system of a society. By constant reiteration these acquired values become internalized and acquire the same status in the image as the biological values—or perhaps even a superior status. The ceremonial life of society largely centers around the reinforcement of the acquired value system. By investitures, coronations, graduations, reunions, and festivals, and even by weddings and funerals, we get together to give ourselves mutual encouragement by the making of solemn affirmations. From early childhood we are surrounded by an impressive symphony of declarations, commandments, dedications, confirmations, resolutions, and reaffirmations. By dint of much speaking the transcript is heard.

It is not by ceremonial and formal instruction alone, however, that value images are created. In our consideration of the dynamics of the value image we must not forget the extreme importance of the small face-to-face group, especially the group of the individual's peers. In every society there seems to be a ceremonial value image which is transmitted by the official and formal institutions of the society; there seems also to be, however, an informal value image which is often much more important in governing the actual behavior of an individual. It is this informal image which is transmitted by the peer group and also very often by the family. The value system of the schoolboy, of the street-corner society, of the student, of the soldier, or of the executive is often markedly different from that which is invoked from the rostrum or sounded from the pulpit. The sanctions of the peer group, however, are usually much more effective on the individual than the sanctions of superiors. This is the basic explanation of the persistence of crime in the face of organized law and the persistence of sin in the face of preaching. We rapidly learn to order our images in the way that the gang orders them because of the extremely low value we place on exclusion and loneliness. We can bear everything except not to be borne by others.

In the intimate face-to-face relationship of the family we find also an important source of acquired values. Because of the dependence of the child on the parent the child quickly learns to value things in the way that the parent does. As in all interpersonal relationships, however, we find in the family too a "vicious dynamic" frequently at work. We are what we are because of the way our parents treated us, because of what they did to us. What parents do to children, however, is very frequently a result of what children do to parents. The child is less socialized, is more of an animal than the parent. It cries when it is hurt, roars when it is angry, and exhibits an unrestrained naturalness of behavior. Any adult who behaved in a way that it is perfectly natural for any child to behave would soon find himself in a mental hospital. He would not be tolerated by society. Because children are children, however, they must be tolerated. The price of this toleration, however, is that they get to be treated in a way that makes them deplorably like their parents when they grow up. So, parents breed parents forever, in a vicious circle which can be broken only by outside forces.

In the last paragraph we have been clearly hovering over the abyss of the Freudian subconscious. Of all the parts of the image the value system is most likely to sink into this underworld where the scanning focus of consciousness cannot penetrate except at twenty-five dollars an hour. Value systems are themselves valued, and the low-valued ones get pushed firmly into the basement and the trapdoor is shut down upon them. There, however, they have their revenge. They devise secret ways of intercepting the messages that come to our doors. They distort the messages which go out from us. They creep up the back stairs at night in our dreams. They frustrate our will. They distort our self-image and ultimately they may destroy our whole personality.

In considering the dynamics of the public image it will not suffice to focus our attention solely on the ceremonial and traditional means of imposing the image. Nor will it suffice to concentrate on the transcript. Nor will it suffice to deal merely with the face-to-face group. All these elements account for the persistence of the image but do not adequately account for its change. To a very large extent change in the image comes about through the impact on society of unusually creative, charismatic, or prophetic individuals. These individuals represent, if we like, mutations in the image. They do not follow in the footsteps of their parents. They question the sanctity of the transcript and they defy the sanctions both of their superiors and of their peers. How these individuals originate and how they exercise their influence on the images of others is a profound mystery. Nevertheless, it is a "fact," that is, it is part of the sophisticated image of society. Often the names and records of these individuals are lost. We know them only by their work. The origin of the images of ancient gods, like the origins of agriculture and the domestication of plants and animals, is lost to record. We can only guess, however, that behind every culture there are heroes. In historic times we know who many of these heroes are. It is not unreasonable that our image of time is studded with great names. Abraham and Moses, Homer and Hesiod, Buddha and Jesus, Paul and Mohammed, Galileo and Newton, Marx and Einstein. Lest we think that all the great are good, let us add Caesar and Constantine and Napoleon and Hitler. These are the "nucleators," the bearers of viable mutant images. These are the founders of nations, churches, societies, businesses, unions, and universities. These are the true entrepreneurs of society.

As in the biological world, we see only the mutants that survive. The world is full of frustrated geniuses, unheard prophets, and unsung heroes, both inside and outside our mental hospitals. Without this mutation of the image, however, society would rapidly settle down to an equilibrium which might not be featureless but which would certainly be stagnant. Many societies, indeed, have done so. Most primitive societies exhibit at least a moderate degree of stability in the image that is transmitted from generation to generation. Even some quite complex civilizations like that of Mohenjo-Daro seem to have been able to suppress all change for nearly a thousand years. Evolution, however, is patient, and change is largely irreversible. We can never go back to any of our Edens. Under the impact of the creative and prophetic powers of the human race the old image constantly changes, giving place to the new. A message comes that speaks with authority reorganizing the images of a whole society from the inside out.

We may not be able to say very much about the appearance of the mutant images. Sometimes the time seems to be ripe and there is no harvester. Sometimes there is a harvester and no harvest. It would seem to carry historical determinism, for instance, to the point of absurdity to argue that if Hitler had had the good fortune to die in infancy another exactly like him would have arisen to perform the function which he performed. Sometimes it is not the single individual but rather the chance combination of individuals which produces the striking effect.

Thus, the sticks which could never burn separately break into a blaze when they are brought together. Had it not been for Saint Paul the history of Christianity would have been greatly different. A Boswell must find his Johnson and the Johnson his Boswell. A Luther must find his princes, a Newton his Royal Society. The talents of many a Gilbert and many a Sullivan must have sputtered out in deserved obscurity because they did not happen to meet the right collaborator.

Nevertheless, in spite of the importance of chance and in spite of the mutational nature of changes in the public image, one cannot avoid the impression that, looking over the long course of recorded history, there is an orderly development in the public image as recorded in the transcript of successive civilizations and generations. We see this very clearly in the spatial image where early images can always be seen as partial and unclear expressions of later and more exact images. From man's image of himself as standing at the center of a small three-storied locality to his image of the four-dimensional relativistic continuum of space and time there is a record of continuous orderly expansion and growth. It is a record characterized by some extravagances and blind alleys. There are still many people who believe that the earth is flat. There are even people who believe that they live on the inside of a hollow sphere. The change in the image comes in mutations, through a Ptolemy, a Copernicus, an Einstein. The over-all development, however, is neither random nor haphazard. The earlier images can almost all be seen as special cases of the later. This is the great test of the developing image in all spheres.

As we trace the image of time also we see a similar orderly development. Here the change in the image takes place mainly through the discovery and development of new records—records in documents, records in rocks, records in carbon 14. The new images, however, are seen as extensions and modifications of the old. The time image of Genesis may be a little weak on measurement, but it is not bad on the order of events!

The relational image likewise exhibits an orderly development through time. We see this most clearly perhaps in mathematics, the purest form of the relational image. New mathematics does not displace the old. The old is almost invariably seen as a special case of the new. Algebra generalizes the operations of arithmetic. The calculus generalizes some operations of algebra. The theory of games is a generalization of the theory of simple maximization. In physics Newtonian mechanics is seen as a special case of the mechanics of relativity. In economics the Keynesian system is easily seen as the generalization of the classical system.

One can hardly escape the impression that the growth of the public image is an orderly process of development, almost one might say from within. The tree of knowledge unfolds in good order and proper succession, first the blade and then the ear, first the trunk and then the branch. It cannot be denied also, however, that the growth of the public image is profoundly affected by disturbances and conditions which are outside the internal structure of this growth. The tree of knowledge may grow from within, but it is also constrained from without. It is bent by storms or encouraged by sunshine in one direction or another. Values are the food of knowledge, and knowledge like any other organism moves toward that part of a possible field of growth where the values are highest. We shall not be surprised, therefore, to find that there is "sociology of knowledge." The messages which come from nature have an urgency, an insistence, and an authority in and of themselves which are not possessed by messages which come from the transcript no matter how weighty the book nor how authoritative the lecturer. It is not surprising, therefore, to find that in an age of clocks Newton fashions the universe in the likeness of an orrery or even that Leibnitz should conceive the incredible notion of the parallel clocks of the physical and mental universes. It is not surprising also that in an age of rapid economic development and extraordinary population increase Darwin should think of evolution and natural selection under conditions of competition and should build an image of the whole history of the earth in the likeness of nineteenth-century England. It is not surprising also that the Bell Telephone Corporation should be the father of information theory or that a world hovering on the edge of automation should produce the science of cybernetics.

All that this means, however, is that the growth of the public image is part and parcel of that larger growth of organization and society. There is no point in getting into a hen versus egg controversy. The egg theory of hens is just as good as the hen theory of eggs. The causal relationships of historical development are too complex to be caught in a catchword.

It is not fanciful, however, to detect pathological relationships at certain times and places in history between the public images and the rest of the social universe. Curiously enough, it is often the most successful images that become the most dangerous. The image becomes institutionalized in the ceremonial and coercive institutions of society. It acquires thereby a spurious stability. As the world moves on, the image does not.

A brief scanning of the historical record calls many such cases to mind. The image of Chinese society became

79

so firmly institutionalized in the family that it took a major revolution to upset it, if it indeed has really been upset. The powerful, unifying, monistic and yet tolerant image of the early days of Islam hardened into a self-perpetuating repressive orthodoxy and a fossil culture. Orthodoxy and capricious power nipped the growing bud of Islam and another branch of human society became the leading shoot. Marxism represents another fossil image, understandable and not wholly unappropriate in its day and capable like Islam of reorganizing whole cultures. Marxism too, however, exhibits marked signs of fossilization. It too has become a sterile orthodoxy maintained by the coercive power of the state.

History is so full of these dead branches of the tree of knowledge that we may well wonder with some trepidation whether our own society will be exempt from what seems to be the almost universal law. There are signs in our own society of a lack of self-confidence in our political images and a desire to maintain them by violence and coercion. This, however, means the cessation of growth. Science is still young. One wonders here also, however, whether this too is not a phase of growth which will come to an end. Science can only flourish in an atmosphere of freedom and uncoerciveness. By its very development, however, the scientific subculture cuts itself off from the society around it. Already there are ominous signs in our society of a revolt against science on the part of those who feel themselves bewildered and frightened by its unintelligible and yet seemingly magical powers.

There are those, of course, who see salvation in the development of the social and behavioral sciences. I cannot, I regret, share this optimism. These sciences can all too easily play into the hands of the manipulators. It is by no means clear that self-consciousness in all things leads to survival, much less to heaven or to Utopia.

It is the vitality, not the particular direction of the tree of knowledge which makes for hope in the whole course of time. It always seems to have a growing shoot somewhere. If one shoot dies another takes over. In growth we trust!

6

The Image in Economic Life

THE ECONOMISTS
have badly neglected the impact of information and
knowledge structures on economic behavior and processes. There are good reasons, or perhaps one should
say excuses, for this neglect. With deft analytical fingers
the economist abstracts from the untidy complexities of
social life a neat world of commodities. It is the behavior
of commodities not the behavior of men which is the
prime focus of interest in economic studies. The economist's world is a world of prices, quantities, interest rates,
production, consumption, income, etc. He studies "the
behavior of prices" (the phrase is actually used by economists) much as the astronomer studies the behavior of
planets. Just as the astronomer, at least before the days of
Einstein, was not particularly interested in the "behavior
of gravity," because gravity was so well behaved it did
not have any behavior, so the economist is not really interested in the behavior of men. He is aware, of course, at
the back of his mind, that prices, outputs, etc., are in fact
the result of human decisions. He likes to reduce these
decisions, however, to a form as abstract and manageable
as possible. Commodities are simple-minded creatures.
In discussing the dynamics of their production, exchange,

and consumption we can assume at least as a first approximation a simple mechanical system which has no need for the concept of an image. Commodities move from where they are cheap to where they are dear. Prices go up when commodities are scarce and come down when they are plentiful.

Even in the simplest theories of economic behavior, however, the concept of an image is latent. Economic behavior is conceived as a process of "maximization." Economic man is supposed to be capable of at least three processes involving an image. In the first place he is supposed to be conscious of the alternatives which lie before him. His image, that is to say, consists of a complex relational image of the form "if I do A then B, C, D, etc. will follow." Or in the simplest form, we suppose his mind to be like a department store full of images of commodities, each with a convenient price ticket attached.

In addition to the image of the alternatives economic man is also supposed to be able to give value-ordering to all relevant alternatives, that is, to all parts of this image. Not only do the combinations of his mental department store have price tags, they have utility tags. What is even more astonishing, all combinations of commodities have utility tags. As the searchlight of his consciousness contemplates five pounds of cheese and a dozen grapefruit it must also reveal whether this particular combination is better or worse than four pounds of cheese and a dozen and a half grapefruit.

His final task after his imagination has performed these labors of Hercules is a simple one. All he needs to do is to scan all possible combinations which are open to him and all his alternative acts, rank them in order on the parade ground of value, and pick out the top of the class. This process of selection of the best alternative is what is known as *maximization* and a great deal of economic theory is built around it. It may be, of course, that the task of economic man is simplified if he is a businessman, by the fact that the whole range of alternatives is supposed to come not with utility tags on them but with profit tags and it is presumably easier to detect that combination which has the largest profit tag than it is to find the combination with the highest utility.

Even as one states the operation of economic behavior, however, as the economist apparently conceives it, one is struck with the extraordinary assumption that it makes about the image. Alternatives do not usually have the courtesy to parade themselves in rank order on the drill ground of the imagination. Our relational image is faulty at the best. Our image of the consequences of our acts is suffused with uncertainty to the point where we are not even sure what we are uncertain about. The economists have tried to deal with the problem of uncertainty by supposing that each of the alternatives in our image presents itself to the mind not only with utility tags attached but also with whole probability distributions. Economic man, clever fellow that he is, now maximizes the expected value of his acts, a feat of mathematical agility which it would take centuries of experience and enormous electronic calculators to perfect.

The situation becomes even worse when we take into account the phenomenon of imperfection in the market. As long as markets are "perfect," the only market information necessary for economic behavior is knowledge of the price of the commodity. In a perfect market the individual can buy or sell as much as he likes of any commodity quoted at the price quoted. The whole range of alternatives open to him in exchange, therefore, is given by the simple information contained in the price

of the commodity and, of course, in his own financial resources. The moment, however, we introduce market
imperfection, which is done increasingly in modern economic theory, the information required of the market for
economic behavior is not a simple price but a whole
schedule or function relating the price of the commodity
to the amount which can be bought or sold. In imperfect
markets it is assumed that the more one sells the smaller
the price that one has to accept, the more one buys the
larger the price one has to offer. It has largely escaped the
attention of economists that the kind of information
required for economic behavior in an imperfect market is
extremely different from that required in a perfect market. In a perfect market the price can be observed, usually posted for anyone to see. It can always be discovered
for the asking. In an imperfect market the function relating price and quantity is nowhere to be observed. All
that can be observed in the market are the prices and
quantities which have prevailed in exchanges in the past
and which are currently prevailing. The prices and quantities which prevailed in the past will only yield information regarding the nature of the price-quantity function
if this function is stable. In a dynamic society, however,
the function rarely is stable. The demand is usually either
increasing or decreasing and hence the experience of the
past gives little information or, indeed, may even give
quite misleading information regarding the potentialities
of the present. The buyer or seller in a perfect market
drives a straight road, the direction of which he can see
for miles ahead or miles behind. The buyer or seller in an
imperfect market drives on a mountain highway where
he cannot see more than a few feet around each curve; he
drives it, moreover, in a dense fog. There is little wonder,
therefore, that he tends not to drive it at all but to stay

where he is. The well-known stability or stickiness of prices in imperfect markets may have much more to do with the uncertain nature of the image involved than with any ideal of maximizing behavior.

There is a large field of investigation open, therefore, in the general area of the nature of economic perception, information, images, and transformation of the image. Consider first the nature of the image of economic alternatives. If we arrange the list of possible actions today in the order of their similarity to what we did yesterday, we are likely to find also that this is an order of certainty or vagueness. If we do on Tuesday what we did on Monday, paying due reverence to the weekly cycle, we know pretty well what the results are going to be. The further we diverge from regular or habitual behavior the less certain are we of the consequences. The larger the negative value that we give to uncertainty or to vagueness in our value orientation, the more likely we are to select the familiar and the known; the more likely we are, therefore, to do today what we did yesterday. This leads to the first revised law of economic behavior: we will do today what we did yesterday unless there are very good reasons for doing otherwise. By a "day" here we mean, of course, the period of regular cyclical activity. We may do this Monday what we did last Monday. We may do on the first of this month what we did on the first of last month. We may do this spring what we did last spring or this Christmas what we did last Christmas, or in this war what we did in the last war. We have here, we may notice, the primitive image of time as an essentially cyclical phenomenon, a time for this and a time for that. A great deal of our behavior even in the complex societies of today is still of this nature. Economic behavior is in no way exempt from this proposition.

86

The second revised law of economic behavior is that the good reasons which are necessary if we do not do today what we did yesterday are derived mainly from dissatisfaction with what we did yesterday or with what happened to us yesterday. In the course of the repetition of habitual activities changes occur in the value structure, that is, in the value image of what we are doing. As we contemplate in good, rational manner the alternatives which are presumably open to us today the likelihood that we will select something else than the habitual pattern depends, of course, upon our satisfaction with this pattern. If we were miserable yesterday we are much more likely to assess the nonhabitual alternative favorably than if we were happy. At some point the misery in the contemplation of the habitual behavior overcomes the uncertainty involved in contemplating any other kind of behavior and we make a reorganization. We quit, we get a new job, we sell out, we buy out. These transformations of the economic image and the subsequent revolutions in behavior seem to come very suddenly. They often represent, however, the culmination of long processes. Discontent builds up slowly with each repetition of habitual behavior until finally we "blow our top," as the utility of the habitual behavior sinks even fractionally below the utility of some possible alternative—a new job, a new location, a new business, perhaps even a new wife.

It is not only the change in the relative value position of the image of the various alternatives which is important in effecting these economic transformations. There are also important changes in the images of the alternatives themselves because of messages received. I am not familiar with any general systematic study of the nature or sources of economic messages. Insofar, however, as all changes in economic alternative-perceptions are the result of messages of some kind or another a study of them seems long overdue. The messages may be, indeed usually are, conveyed through some kind of a transcript—the newspaper, the financial pages, the market reports, the ticker tape, the news broadcasts, etc. A broad study of the readership and impact of messages of this kind is badly needed. We must not neglect, however, in considering the formation of economic images, the part played by personal or face-to-face messages. In determining the flow of migration of peoples from areas of less to areas of greater economic opportunity, for instance, the part played by the personal messages probably overshadows by far the influence of the public transcript. It is not the propaganda of the chambers of commerce that brings people to California; it is the letter or even more the visit from the enthusiastic friends or relatives who have moved west and found the "pickings" good. A great part of the general migration of European peoples to the areas of colonization may be explained in like manner.

One suspects, although we have no studies of this, that face-to-face or personal messages are of great importance even in the determination of business decisions. This is because a personal message always carries more "weight" than an impersonal one. The nauseating and usually self-defeating efforts of advertisers to "personalize" their communications is testimony to the truth of this proposition. The gossip in the club and on the golf course may be of much more importance in effecting radical reorganizations of the image of alternatives in the minds even of quite responsible and important businessmen than is sometimes imagined.

The image of the alternatives may have several characteristics or dimensions. There is, for instance, a general dimension of "optimism" or "pessimism." Forty years ago Professor Pigou attributed the phenomenon of the business cycle largely to waves of optimism and pessimism transmitted through the business community by face-to-face communication. The dynamics of these waves of optimism and pessimism is little understood and needs to be investigated from the point of view of the information-image complex. Besides the general character of optimism or pessimism the image of the alternatives will also contain important specific characteristics, some of which may be quite peculiar to the individual concerned. A manufacturer, for instance, may be rather generally pessimistic as a result of the long faces he has observed at the club, but he may also have a confidential report on his table regarding an unusually favorable opportunity in some location. There is an interesting field of study also in what might be called "symbolic" public messages. Certain institutions like the stock market get to have a reputation for being the bellwether of general economic conditions. A collapse of prices on the stock market, therefore, is likely to be interpreted in a way that will increase the pessimism of most images quite apart from any necessary connection between the message received and the alternatives contemplated.

The development of public information and economic indices is also of great importance in assessing the effect of messages on the economic image. The economic consequences of this rapid spread of information have never been adequately assessed. Not only the publications of the Department of Commerce, but the outpourings of many private business soothsayers are scanned eagerly by those who are responsible for important decisions. It is significant, incidentally, in the light of the message-image relationship that the "personalized" typewritten or mimeographed sheet apparently exercises greater authority than the printed page. We seem to be reaching the stage where a scribbled note on yellow paper would command the highest authority of all. We may recall, for instance, the devious devices of Daniel Drew, who would conceal false notes to his brokers in his hat; notes which would flutter to the floor of the exchange after a gesture of politeness, there to be scrambled for eagerly by the soon-to-be-frustrated inside-dopesters.

The process of reorganization of economic images through messages is the key to the understanding of economic dynamics. The great over-all processes of economic life—inflation, deflation, depression, recovery, and economic development are governed largely by the process of reorganization of economic images through the transmission of messages. One may hazard a guess that one of the main determinants of the rate of these processes is the rate of transmission of the messages which govern them. Other things being equal, the faster messages move the faster their effect will be felt. A change which might take a generation to accomplish in a slow-moving non-literate society may be accomplished in months or even days in a society favored with mass communication and the almost instantaneous transmission of information from place to place. This generalization, however, must not be carried too far; it is not the message that is important but the transformation of the image which it produces. A society may have very rapid transmission of messages yet if its images are stable and resist the impact of the messages change will be slow no matter how swiftly the messages themselves course through the channels of communication.

Let us consider, for instance, the process by which the transmission of messages and the subsequent reorganization of images may create in society a process of deflation and depression. Suppose, for instance, that we postulate some initiating unfavorable event such as a stock market crash or the failure of a prominent bank. This may create, because of the rapid spread of public messages through the mass media, a certain predisposition to pessimism throughout the whole society. This means that messages which previously might be interpreted as nonsignificant or random variations are now interpreted in a pessimistic way. A manufacturer, for instance, receives information that his sales have not quite come up to what he expected and that his inventories are piling up. If the general mood of the society were optimistic this might result in little more than the calling of a salesmen's conference and a pep talk. If there is, however, a pessimistic predisposition this information may be received as confirmation that things are going to be bad, and the result is a cutback in output, the dismissal of men, etc. The reduction of output automatically reduces income, the reduction of income automatically reduces sales of other commodities, and other manufacturers find themselves plagued with the same situation and may make the same response. Every time a message is interpreted as a signal to cut back output this creates messages in other parts of the system which may have the same effect. As the general pessimism grows there is an increasing preference for money and liquid assets and an increasing reluctance to engage in productive processes or to hold "real" assets. The greater this reluctance the more it is justified. The message system operates here in a kind of vicious spiral with the reactions to messages in one part of the system confirming the messages in other parts. There comes to be a widespread image of the future in terms of declining prices. This leads to an unwillingness to buy, an over-eagerness to sell. The way to get rich, of course, in a period of declining prices is to sell all you have and hold on to the proceeds until the bottom of the decline is reached. If everybody tries to do this, however, the price decline will be catastrophic. A similar dynamic process may also be traced for recovery. It may also be traced for inflation.

Another problem which cannot be solved without the intervention of the idea of an image and of the modification of the image by messages, is the problem of "oligopoly" or of competition among the few. The image in this case is of peculiar complexion because it has to include not only a simple notion of the consequences of one's acts; it must also include an image of the reactions of others to one's acts, because the consequences of one's acts depend on the reactions of one's competitors. Conditions as far apart as the continual price wars or almost uninterrupted price stability may result from what is essentially the same market condition, depending on the nature of the images of the participants. Where the image is a short-range one, where the reactions of one's own behavior on others are little regarded or thought of as unimportant, the "price war" condition is likely. The market situation here is where we have a few firms selling identical products. A price cut on the part of one of them which does not produce an immediate response from the others may result in a very large transfer of custom toward the price-cutting firm. If, however, the other firms meet the price of the price-cutter they are able to attract their old custom back to themselves and all firms are left with approximately the same share of the market but all are worse off than before. If, however, the image of all the firms is an extended and sophisticated one so that each firm realizes that any benefit which accrues to it from a price cut will only be temporary, the temptation to cut prices is much less and we may have highly stable situations, even without any formal agreement. There is an almost exact analogue of this situation in the international arms race which will be discussed in the next chapter.

The problem of the transformation of images is of great importance in the theory of economic development. It may be indeed that the rather unsatisfactory state of the theory of economic development at the present time is a direct result of the failure to build into it a theory of the image. The problem here is that of the initiation and imitation of superior processes. Both these phenomena require transformation of the image; a new process always starts as a new image, as a new idea. The process itself is merely a form of transcription of the new image. Frequently, the images involved are extremely complex relational images, the establishment of which is by no means easy. Consider, for instance, the problems involved in persuading a traditionally pastoral people to use the plow. Their previous image is one in which the life-giving grass grows spontaneously over the landscape and is preserved and utilized to feed the livestock on which the whole society depends. The very first step of the new process is to plow the grass under, to destroy the familiar life-giving green carpet and replace it by a waste of barren earth. Not until the seed is planted, is grown, and yields its crop, will the new image be firmly implanted and in the meantime the old image which has served generation upon generation must ruthlessly be destroyed or devalued.

The problem of the initiation of technical change is a much more puzzling one than would seem at first sight. We are so accustomed to change in our society and have institutionalized it to so great an extent that we do not realize what a rare, difficult, and utterly incomprehensible phenomenon it is. Any change from settled ways of life involves a fearful plunge into the unknown. It will not be undertaken unless either there is great dissatisfaction with the existing routine or unless there is something in the society which puts a high positive value on change itself. Then the question arises: Where does the original message come from which brings about the original reorganization of the image? It is not difficult to understand the spread or repetition of an image once it has been established. There will be powerful messages issuing from the pioneers who have tried the new method and found it successful, and these messages can easily reorganize the images of the laggards. If a totally new image is to come into being, however, there must be sensitivity to internal messages, the image itself must be sensitive to change, must be unstable, and it must include a value image which places high value on trials, experiments, and the trying of new things. The internal stability of traditional societies is a direct result of the sanctions which they place against novelty. Yet it seems almost of the essence of society to impose such sanctions, and one wonders how conditions ever arise in which these sanctions can be broken.

A guess may be hazarded that one of the important conditions for the initiation of technological change is the development of rather isolated and perhaps somewhat persecuted subcultures within the larger society. It is in the "nonconformist" subcultures that images are most likely to be sensitive and subject to change. The fact that the subculture itself puts a high value on revolt against the orthodoxy of the society also leaves it open to revolt against the orthodoxy of the present. This proposition can be well documented in the period of the industrial revolution where most of the major changes were in fact made by nonconformists, that is, by people who belonged to nonconforming subcultures within the larger society. It is impossible to document this for the earlier technological revolution, such as the domestication of plants and livestock and the invention of agriculture. It may not be accidental, however, that all the early civilizations seem to have been theocracies, rising first perhaps as dissident subcultures in the traditional and "pagan" world around them.

The course of economic development also depends largely on what I have earlier called the "tree of knowledge." Images like other organizations have an embryology; they start off by being simple, they grow and they develop and as they develop they become increasingly complex. At each stage of development, therefore, there are only certain alternative ways of development open; everything builds on what has gone before. Sometimes, indeed, the development of technical knowledge requires the coming together at a particular period in history of many diverse branches of knowledge and skill. The automobile seems to represent such a nodal point in technical development. One can point to many techniques without which the automobile would have been impossible; there had to be an internal combustion engine, there had to be techniques of refining gasoline, there had to be techniques for handling rubber, there had to be electric batteries and spark plugs, there had to be the ability to make good roads. Only the roads we might have had earlier had there been the incentive. In a very real sense the automobile created the roads on which we drive. The automobile itself could hardly have been invented at any period in history apart from the end of the nineteenth century. At the end of the nineteenth century, however, it could hardly help being invented;

all the parts had come together and the fact that so many different makes of automobiles were invented in the early days indicates that something would have happened even had it not been for the genius of Henry Ford. It can be said also that the development of atomic energy would never have taken place had it not been for the development of organizational skills in the previous two generations. Here again many different kinds of development converge.

7

The Image in the Political Process

JUST AS THE TRADITIONAL
subject matter of economics is wealth, that is, commodities, so the traditional subject matter of political science is power. In the case of economics we saw that it is possible to develop quite elaborate abstract models without the explicit concepts of the image. This is—to quote Jevons—"the mechanics of utility and self-interest." We saw also, however, that if this abstraction is to go beyond the level of very first approximation, we must introduce the image-forming process in society. If we are to have a theory of economic behavior or a theory of economic dynamics an explicit recognition of the importance of the image is necessary.

Political science has never succeeded in developing an adequate theoretical system on purely mechanical lines. From this point of view the concept of power has not turned out to be a useful abstraction in spite of the fact that it was originally derived from mechanics. The power that is the subject matter of political science is so unlike the power concept as used in classical mechanics that not even the first approximation of the political process has been derived from mechanical models. In this area, therefore, one may venture the hope that the concept of the image and the image-forming process in society will enable us to develop a first approximation theory of the political process—a first approximation which up to now has been sadly lacking.

The question is, out of the general view of the social process which we have developed in these chapters, a view which sees the whole movement of society as a process of image-formation under the stimulus of messages transmitted by networks of communication: Can we abstract or identify something which might be called a political process? I believe the answer to this question is "yes." We can identify first of all a problem of decision-making in groups or organizations. We have seen that for purposes of the theory of organization we must break up the individual person into a number of roles. One of the important dimensions of the role is the private-public dimension. This is largely a question of the image of the organization into which the role is seen to fit. There is an obvious difference between the kind of decision which is made by an individual out for a solitary walk as to whether he should take the right path or the left, and the kind of decision which is made by the leader of a large organization in matters of high policy. In the first case, the decision affects no one presumably but the decider; in the second case, the decision of a single individual may have profound effects on the lives of millions. By the "power" of a role, therefore, we mean the number of people affected and the magnitude of the effect when decisions are made.

The political process then may be abstracted from the general processes of social life by concentrating on the processes by which these "public" decisions are made. This is not the whole story, however. We are also interested not only in how public decisions are made, but in who makes them. We are interested in what determines the structure of powerful roles in society and we are also interested in the processes by which these roles are filled.

Let us consider first the decision-making process itself in group organizations. It is customary to think of the structure of organizations in terms of a dimension of authoritarianism and democracy. The structural difference is reflected partly in a difference of the role-images involved and also in a difference in the lines of communication. In the ideal type of the authoritarian system we have a strict hierarchy of roles, each role-image containing the expectation of subordination to higher roles and authority over lower roles. Decisions originate with the higher roles and are transmitted to the lower roles as orders. The lower roles are expected to execute the orders without any back-talk. Information is transmitted from lower roles to higher roles on request of the higher role. All decisions originate at the top and are transmitted downward, where they are supposed to be executed in acts. The information which ascends the role structure is supposed to be feedback from these acts. The form of the information, however, is governed from above not from below. It is not volunteered, it is requested.

At the other end of the scale we have the ideal type of the democratic organization. Even in this we can still distinguish between the higher roles and the lower roles and between leaders and followers. Authority, however, is now supposed to proceed from below. The higher roles are supposed to act on behalf of and to be responsible to the lower roles. What this means in practice is that the decisions of the higher roles have to be made by discussion. That is to say, hypothetical decisions are made and communicated to the lower roles. The lower roles react to these hypothetical decisions and as a result of these feedbacks the decisions are modified until substantial agreement is reached—the discussion proceeds until the high roles announce the decision which receives the approval of the lower ones or at least of a majority of them. There may be different conventions of what constitutes approval—majority rule is only one of these, and it does not constitute an essential part of the democratic process.

It may be seen from the above descriptions that the principal difference between the two ideal models lies in the different nature of the feedback to the higher roles. In the authoritarian model the feedback is indirect and is to a considerable extent under the control of the higher roles themselves. In the democratic model the feedback is much more direct and has a more powerful influence in the modification of decisions. We may perhaps hazard the suggestion that there is some optimum degree of feedback from the lower to the higher roles, and that this is perhaps a more important notion than a strict dichotomised image of the political process as divided sharply into authoritarian and democratic structures. The weakness of the authoritarian structure lies in the inadequate amount of feedback to the higher roles because the tyrant controls his sources of information. These sources become increasingly unreliable. He tends to surround himself with "yes men" and hence his image of the world becomes increasingly divorced from the image of the lower roles. This leads to increasing strain and dissatisfaction within the organization until, finally, there is a revolution and the tyrant is dethroned. The authoritarian structure is only possible as long as the image of the lower roles possessed by the persons occupying them includes an element of acceptance of the structure itself. In the absence of any adequate information system from the bottom up, the higher roles find themselves eventually incapable of maintaining this acceptance of their position. The image which is possessed by the higher roles of the images of the lower roles becomes increasingly unreal. They see loyalty where there is none, or what is even worse, they see treachery where there is none, and eventually the whole complex of images and of images of images then becomes incapable of supporting itself and the organization disintegrates.

There is a strong tendency for authoritarian organizations to use violence or the threat of violence in support of the role structure, that is, in order to gain acceptance of the role on the part of the persons occupying the lower role. For a time this may be successful in maintaining the organization. It is usually, however, self-defeating because of the corruption of the communication system which it entails. The case is somewhat analogous to that of the schizophrenic or the extreme paranoid. His sense receptors are so much "afraid" of him that they merely confirm the products of his heated imagination. The terrorized information sources of the tyrant likewise tell him only what they think will be pleasing to his ears. Organizations as well as individuals can suffer from hallucinations. It is the peculiar disease of authoritarian structures.

At the other extreme, democratic structures in which there is no adequate leadership, that is, in which the feedback is destructive of the decision-making process on the part of higher roles are likewise unstable and incapable of maintaining themselves. If discussion is to be a successful process of decision-making it must exhibit a degree of convergence toward common images of the whole organization. If the feedback from the followers destroys the image of the leader instead of merely modifying it, the process is likely to be self-defeating. The leader will cease to be respected or accepted. Many would-be leaders aspire to the role, there is a conflict among leaders, and the process can easily degenerate into anarchy. It is the object of what might be called the paraphernalia of democratic organizations: the elections, the rules of order, the parliamentary procedure, etc., to establish what might be called an image of conventional leadership. These procedures are by no means always successful, and when they break down, there is a certain tendency for organizations to slip back into authoritarian forms. It may be argued, indeed, that both democratic and authoritarian forms are inherently unstable, and that the general political dynamic consists of an oscillation between the two.

The view of the political process which I have outlined above, which regards it as a process of mutual modification of images through the processes of feedback and communication, is in marked contrast to certain conventional views of the democratic process. In the conventional view, the democratic process is regarded as a summation, indexing, or resolution of individual preferences. This view leads to the so-called "voting paradoxes" and the "Arrow dilemma." This is the view put forth by Kenneth Arrow: that it is impossible to construct a social welfare function, that is, an ordering of possible alternatives by any process of the summation of the individual preference functions of the members of the society—impossible, that is to say, except under certain very unlikely or undesirable conditions. This seems to be a completely unreal model of the nature of the political process, which is not that of the summation of fixed individual preferences but is the process of the mutual modification of images both relational and evaluational in the course of mutual communication, discussion, and discourse. The course of the discussion is punctuated by decisions which are essentially temporary in nature in the sense that they do not close the discussion, although they do, of course, have the effect of modifying it. In one sense, in a successful political process all decisions are interim. We live in a perpetual state of unresolved conflict. A decision is a partial resolution of conflict. It should never be a complete resolution. The majority does not rule; a majority decision is simply a setting of the terms under which the minority continues the discussion—a discussion which presumably goes on forever or at least for the lifetime of the organization. We need careful study of the way in which the communication networks of organizations affect not only the distribution of images of the role but also affect the value structures of the individuals concerned. Only thus will we come to a real understanding of the decision-making process.

The dynamics of political life can be interpreted largely in terms of the interaction of two processes. The first is the process whereby political images are created and distributed among the individuals of a society. The second is the process whereby specialized skills and knowledge are distributed among the people of the society. The political image is essentially an image of roles. Consider, for instance, the picture that we have of the American presidency. This is a role image which originated in the minds of the founding fathers and in the course of the long political and constitutional discussions which preceded the founding of this republic. It is an image which is partly enshrined in the transcript of the Constitution. It is an image, however, which has been changing slowly in the course of history and which is derived in part from the recorded experience of the occupants of the role. The role is the center of a complex network of communications both in and out, part of which each occupant of the role inherits and a part of which he creates for himself. It is an essential part of the image of the role that the occupant should be selected by a national election and that he should terminate the role at a stated date, unless, of course, he is re-elected. The occupant of the role is expected to be affable and accessible; he is expected to shake hands with innumerable people; he is expected to sign his name to innumerable documents; he is expected to make public pronouncements on important occasions; and he has large numbers of rights and duties prescribed to him both by the formal and informal constitution. An image of this role is present in the minds of millions of Americans in greater or less degree of clarity. It is not only present, it is accepted, that is, it is placed high on the value scale. The image, both in its behavioral aspects and in its value aspects, is perpetuated from generation to generation partly through the agencies of formal instruction, even more perhaps through the informal face-to-face communication between parents and child or among peers. The image of the role is so strong that it has a profound influence on its occupants. Men who previously have been rather commonplace, uninspired, perhaps even rather dubious characters under the influence of the role become "Mr. President" rather than Joe Doakes. Each individual as he occupies the role, however, leaves to some extent his own impress upon it. Great men ennoble the roles which they take; little men debase them.

The whole of society is permeated with these images of political roles. We must look for them not only in what are ordinarily thought of as political organizations such as the state, the federal government, or the local political unit. The political role, the political image is to be found in all organizations, even in organizations as small as the family. The business firm, the church, the school, the university, the foundation, the orphanage, the trade union, the lodge, the club, all consist of a structure of political images—presidents, vice-presidents, secretary-treasurers, committeemen, legislators, elder statesmen, branch managers, foremen, etc., on down to busboys. Each person has an image not only of his own role, but of a great many roles around him. These images are constantly being changed by the messages received. They are changed by confirmations and disappointments; they are perpetuated by ritual observances and established lines of communication. We might hazard a proposition, for instance, that in those organizations where acceptance of the role is small, the role must be reinforced by extensive and elaborate forms of ceremonial behavior. This is particularly apt to be true of authoritarian structures such as the armed forces or the authoritarian churches. Armies are full of people who do not really want to do what they are doing and who are coerced into accepting the role in which they are placed. Under these circumstances, it is necessary to reinforce the role by an elaborate system of ceremonial behavior, saluting, spit and polish, and the like.

Over against the process by which the distribution of images of roles is established in society, there is another process which determines the distribution of specialized skills and knowledge. All roles require certain degrees of skill in the performance of the role as well as an image of the role itself. If the role is occupied by individuals who do not have the requisite skills, the image of the role is profoundly modified in all those with whom they come into contact. We may think perhaps of the distribution of knowledge and skill in society as corresponding to some "normal" structure of role images in which a role corresponds to every skill. The actual distribution of role images differs, of course, from this normal distribution. High places are occupied by nincompoops and many a flower of skill and intellect is born to blush unseen. Wherever, however, high places are occupied by those who do not have the requisite skills and where low places are occupied by those who have the high skills, the situation is profoundly unstable. The distribution of skills is continually upsetting the distribution of roles. One may say, therefore, as a long-run tendency that the distribution of power in society is mainly a function of the distribution of skills. It is the dynamics of the distribution of skill which forms, as it were, the long swell on which the shifts of power occur as minor ups and downs. Hence, the long-run dynamics of the distribution of power can only be understood as a byproduct of the more fundamental dynamics of the distribution of skill.

The two processes are not, of course, unrelated. Part of the power of the powerful is power over the acquisition of skill. A ruling class may keep its power for a very long time by the proper manipulation of the sources of acquired skill. This it may do partly by the monopoly of formal education, and partly by the subtle processes of face-to-face transfer by which the children of the ruling class grow up in the ruling class and learn the skills of the ruling class, not only the know-how, but also the "know-whom." If the ruling class is too small and too inbred, it may suffer from genetic deterioration. If it is able, however, to maintain a continued infiltration of genetic elements from below, on the representatives of which it imposes its own cultural stamp, it may persist for many generations.

As independent sources of skill develop, however,

especially with the increase in the division of labor in society, it becomes increasingly difficult to establish any monopoly in the sources of acquired skill. This would seem to be the grain of truth in the Marxist view of history as an ecological succession of classes. As the market widens, and commerce grows, for instance, a specialized class of merchants develops whose skills are foreign to those of the aristocracy. In a mercantile society the skill of the merchant is an essential ingredient of the conduct of a state. Power eventually follows the skill, and the mercantile class either displaces the old ruling class or becomes associated with it. The Marxist interpretation, however, rests on a wholly inadequate mechanical analogy. Once we see society as a process of modification of images through messages, it becomes clear that there is no mechanical process of overthrow of one class by the one below it. Instead, there is a much more complex process whereby the dynamics of the political image and of the distribution of skill and knowledge interact.

The rise of modern technology and the growth in the complexity of the knowledge structure of the society is perhaps the dominant factor in the political process of modern times. In a society as complex as ours, there is no possibility of establishing monopolies of the sources of skill. Feudal, monarchical, or aristocratic societies, therefore, which depend for their maintenance on the transmission of a monopoly of skills from one generation of the elite to the next, are doomed. Either they must reject economic development, in which case they lose their external power position in the international scene, or if they accept economic development, the aristocratic structure becomes unstable.

An excellent example of the impotence of formal political "power" in the face of inappropriate distributions of skill is to be found in the recent history of Great Britain. We there saw the spectacle of a would-be socialist government quite incapable of effecting any real transfers of power from the existing managers of large-scale industry. The steel industry, for instance, has to be run by the people who know how to make steel. This skill, however, is acquired not by winning elections, but by growing up in the midst of steelmen. It is this "node" of scarce knowledge which constitutes the real power-structure of the society, and all the political and parliamentary mechanisms were quite unable to alter this fact. It is for this reason, for instance, that the rise of the labor movement actually presents only a very small challenge to the power of the managerial group. The skill by which a man attains control of the labor union is not the same skill by which he operates a business. As long as this is the case, the managerial class is relatively safe.

An extremely interesting problem is presented by the relation between the dynamics of power and the dynamics of skill under communism. In the United States the popular image of communism is that of a monolithic tyranny capable of maintaining itself in a more or less unchanged form indefinitely. It may well be, however, that because of the conflict between the two dynamic processes we have outlined, authoritarian, monolithic communism is highly unstable in a period of rapidly expanding technological skill. The image of the dictatorship of the proletariat is a myth of considerable power. Nevertheless, it is a myth which is so unrelated to the dynamics of knowledge and skill that it is unlikely to be very stable. It seems likely that authoritarian forms of organizational structure are quite inappropriate in developing the kinds of skill which a highly technological society requires. Within the structure of American business enterprises, for instance, we have seen a marked change in the present generation from highly authoritarian structures toward looser and more democratic ones, with greater decentralization of power and distribution of authority, human relations programs, and the like. In the communist world also, there may be a profound tendency toward the replacement of authoritarian structures by looser and more democratic ones. Because of the imperious demands of the dynamics of skill, we are rapidly approaching the time when labor as brute force, mechanically applied, will become obsolete. As we move forward into the society of the skilled, such a society would seem necessarily to be based on extensive discussion, accurate feedbacks, a network of mutual information channels, and an absence of coercion. This is close to our ideal image of democracy.

It does not do, of course, to be too optimistic. There is a very real dilemma of power in society in that the images which are useful in gaining power are seldom useful in exercising it wisely or in keeping it. In formal democracies the ability to get elected is not identical with the ability to govern wisely. We are still far from solving the problem of devising a political institution which will at the same time permit extensive discussion and optimum feedbacks and minimize coercion on the one hand, and yet will also insure that the skills which lead to the attainment of the leadership roles are also identical with the skills required in performing these roles.

Political images include not only detailed images of role expectations. They also include what might be called symbolic or personalized images of institutions themselves. A symbolic image is a kind of rough summation or index of a vast complexity of images of roles and structures. These symbolic images are of great importance in political life, and especially in international relations. We think of the United States, for instance, as Uncle Sam; of England as John Bull; or of Russia as a performing bear. These symbolic images are particularly important in the summation and presentation of value images. Value images do not usually consist of a long and detailed list of alternatives in a carefully compiled rank-order. They consist, rather, of a "posture" which in a sense summarizes an extremely complex network of alternatives and situations. In Christianity, for instance, the symbol of the Crucifix or of the Virgin has exercised an enormous evocative power through the centuries because of the way in which these symbols summarize a whole value system, a whole attitude toward life and the universe. Political images do the same thing at a different level. The creators of these symbolic images exercise quite extraordinary power over the imaginations of men and the course of events. Consider, for example, the power of the image of the political party in the United States. The Republican Party is conceived as an elephant, rather old, rather dignified, a little slow, not perhaps terribly bright, but with a good deal of wisdom, hard working, full of integrity, rather conservative, a little isolated from the world around him, patient, thick-skinned, but capable of occasional inarticulate squeals of rage. The Democratic Party is thought of as a donkey, active, agile, clever, a little unsure of himself, a bit of an upstart, quick, sensitive, a little vulgar, and cheerfully absurd. These images are reiterated by cartoons and have been of great importance in establishing the political climate.

In international relations, the symbolic image of the nation is of extraordinary importance. Indeed, it can be argued that it has developed to the point where it has become seriously pathological in its extreme form. The national symbol becomes the object of a kind of totem-worship. Cartoons and political speeches continually reinforce the image of roles of nations as "real" personalities—lions, bears, and eagles, loving, hating, embracing, rejecting, quarreling, fighting. By these symbols, the web of conflict is visualized not as a shifting, evanescent, unstable network of fine individual threads but as a simple tug-of-war between large opposing elements. This symbolic image is one of the major causes of international warfare and is the principal threat to the survival of our present world.

It must not be thought, of course, that symbolic images are all "bad." Indeed, the symbolic image is absolutely necessary as a part of the economy of image-formation. The human imagination can only bear a certain degree of complexity. When the complexity becomes intolerable, it retreats into symbolic images. We have an intense hatred, for instance, of multidimensional value orderings. We cannot be content, for instance, by saying that John is better than Bill in mathematics but worse in history. We want to put John and Bill on a single linear scale and say, at the end of the year, John is "better" than Bill—or vice-versa. In order to do this, however, we must do a certain violence to the complexity of the value-structure. This injury is the price that we pay for simplicity. Similarly, in political life it is impossible to vote for the "good" and against the "bad." What we are always voting for are complex bundles, like John and Bill. If we are very keen on mathematics, we vote for John. If we prefer history, we vote for Bill. The instability of voting behavior is a result of the complexity of the detailed image which is summarized in the symbol. Small changes in our detailed valuations may make all the difference between preferring one symbol and preferring another.

One important clue to the dynamics of international relations is the fact that the symbolic image of the nation has important dimensions of security and insecurity. It is this fact that leads, under certain circumstances, to the disastrous phenomenon of the arms race. We saw, in the previous chapter, how competition among a few business firms could lead either to a situation of price warfare or a situation of extreme price stability depending on the nature of the image (that is essentially of the symbolic image) held by each firm of the others and of itself. An exactly similar proposition may be stated in international relations. The symbolic image of one's own nation is tinged with ideas of security or insecurity depending on one's image of other nations. In the image of the United States today, for instance, possessed by the majority of its people, there is a strong overtone of insecurity produced by their image of the Soviet Union as an aggressive, expanding power. Because of this image, the United States undertakes policies and performs actions which lead to the establishment or the reinforcement of an image in the Soviet Union, mistaken as it may be, of the United States as an aggressive, expanding power. If national policy depends mainly on the present image of the nation and not on the changes in the image which may be visualized as a result of the consequences of action, a highly unstable situation develops. A nation perceives itself as insecure and, hence, increases its armaments or maintains an aggressive posture. By doing so, it seeks to increase its image of its own security. In so doing, however, it diminishes the security in the image of its opponent. The security of one is the insecurity of the other.

We have then a vicious process which goes something

like this: A feels insecure and hence increases its armaments; this makes B feel insecure and so B increases its armaments; this makes A feel insecure again, so A increases its armaments; this makes B feel insecure again, so B increases its armaments. This process may go on until either a war breaks out because one party or the other finds the situation intolerable or some other change occurs which reverses the process. We thus see that the cycle of war and peace is not wholly dissimilar in form from the business cycle. Just as in economic life we can trace dynamic processes of recovery on the one hand in which things go from worse to better, and recession on the other when things go from better to worse, so in the sphere of international relations we can distinguish two opposing processes. We have on the one hand the "postwar" periods in which, on the whole, things go from worse to better, and we have the "prewar" periods in which things go from better to worse. Just as in economic life, so in international relations there are mysterious turning points. Recessions do not always result in a major crisis, nor do prewar periods always result in a war. There may be spontaneous changes in the image which will reverse each of these processes. We may venture on the proposition, however, that the more complex and extended the image possessed by each nation of itself and the others, the less likely are we to find vicious dynamic processes of the arms-race type. When nations cease to think of their security in absolute terms, when they begin to evaluate the effect of any increase in their own arms on the armaments of others, then we are more likely to develop processes of interaction which lead to mutual trust rather than to mutual suspicion. The problem of discovering the appropriate institutions which will guarantee benevolent rather than vicious dynamic processes in international relations is still very far from being solved. Nevertheless, if we think of it in these terms, rather than in the formal terms of protocol, constitution, and procedure, we will be that much nearer a solution.

Much needs to be done in the study of the creation of symbolic images. There can be little doubt that poets, historians, writers, and cartoonists play an enormous role in the development of these images. There is some truth in the claim that nations are the creation of their historians—it is the image of the past that gives rise both to the image of the present and of the future. The British school boy is drilled incessantly in the glories of rascally old pirates like Drake, and his heart heaves with pride at the sentimental histrionics of a Nelson. The American school boy is similarly indoctrinated with the glories of John Paul Jones and the achievements of the "Monitor" or the "Merrimac," depending, of course, on which side of the Mason-Dixon line he happens to live. It is an instructive lesson in history to compare the accounts of the War of 1812 in Canadian and American textbooks, especially those prepared for the impressionable minds of the young.

Here again however, the transcript is not the whole story. The nation is an older invention than either the textbook or the mass medium. It is perhaps the shared experience of danger which more than anything else creates the national spirit. Nations are the creation not of their historians, but of their enemies. France is a creation of Germany, and Germany of France. In the twentieth century the "perishing republic hardening into empire" of the United States is partly the creation of Russia, and the neurotic, aggressive Russia is partly the creation of the United States. We still await the larger symbolic image which will unite us all.

8

How Manifest Is Destiny?
The Image in History

I NOW WISH TO RETURN
to a theme which has been hinted at several times in the
course of this discussion. I have suggested that one of the
basic theorems of the theory of the image is that it is
the image which in fact determines what might be called
the current behavior of any organism or organization.
The image acts as a field. The behavior consists in gravi-
tating toward the most highly valued part of the field. It
does not follow from this, however, that the consequences
of behavior are in conformity with the image which produced them. Disappointment and surprise are a common
lot of both organisms and organizations. We behave according to some image of the consequences of our acts.
When, however, these consequences are reflected in information fed back to us, we find very often that feedback
does not confirm the original image. Under these circumstances, as we have seen, the image may be modified or it
may not. What we are concerned with in this chapter,
however, is not so much modification of the image by
disappointment, as the relationship between those processes in the history both of the individual and of society
which seem to be relatively independent of the images

held and those processes which are sharply dependent on the image. The first processes are called "latent," the second processes are the "manifest." The relation of manifest to latent processes, both in the development of the individual and in the history of society, is perhaps the most interesting question in the theory of history.

The distinction between the latent and the manifest needs further exploration before we proceed. We have in the first place processes taking place both in the individual and in society which are quite independent of any images held. These might be described as the mechanical latent processes as they involve essentially mechanical models which are quite independent of the information-message-image complex. In the human individual the processes of growth, physical development, and aging are almost entirely of this latent type. "What man by taking thought can add a cubit to his stature?" The growth and decay of the body seem to be processes almost completely independent of the nature or quality of our image either conscious or unconscious. There may be a few subtle relationships here of which we are not at present aware. It will be very surprising if they are very firm or very stable. If we jump off a skyscraper, no matter how elevated our thoughts on the way down, they will hardly affect the rapidity of our descent or the consequences at the bottom.

There are social processes also which partake of this nature. The geographical location of human activity is in part, at any rate, a result of forces quite outside either the conscious or the unconscious image of mankind. We do not expect the Eskimos to grow tropical fruit; we cannot mine coal where there is no coal or develop water power in the desert. The location of cities is in part a result of the accidents of history and of human institutions.

Still, the plain physical shape of the earth has a good deal to do with the location of most of them. It is by no means an accident that New York is located on an excellent harbor with easy access to the interior of the country or that Chicago is the focus of a fine geographical bottleneck produced by the Great Lakes.

It is surprisingly difficult, however, to find processes in human history which are truly mechanically latent in the sense that they are quite independent of any image which may be held by the people participating in them. The mutations which may be caused by the increase in atomic radiation are perhaps a good example.

Although it is difficult to find processes in society which exhibit a mechanical latency in a pure form, there are many models of social processes in which the nature of the image is so unimportant that it can be neglected. Some of these part-mechanical models throw real light on actual social history. A good example of these quasi-latent models is the Malthusian theory. This is the famous dismal theorem of economics that if the only check on the growth of population is starvation and misery, then no matter how favorable the environment or how advanced the technology the population will grow until it is miserable and starves. The theorem, indeed, has a worse corollary which has been described as the utterly dismal theorem. This is the proposition that if the only check on the growth of population is starvation and misery, then any technological improvement will have the ultimate effect of increasing the sum of human misery, as it permits a larger population to live in precisely the same state of misery and starvation as before the change.

There are enough known examples of the operations of Malthusian systems in history to make the model highly relevant even in the present day. The latent nature of the process depends on the fact that the images which are involved in the procreative process seldom have relevance to the future prosperity of the society in which the individual is involved. Where the reproduction of the species is purely the result of sexual gratification as it is in all the lower animals, the process of reproduction and survival might be described as completely latent. The image which gives rise to sexual behavior has no relation whatever to the consequences, especially the ultimate consequences of that behavior. In the human race, this pristine latency is somewhat impaired by the fact that there is foresight and that contraception is possible, at least in the sense of some disassociation of the sexual act from its progenitive consequences. Even though the consequences of the acts may be manifest for the individual, however, they are frequently latent for the society at large. The individual may welcome children because of their economic value to him, but what is a gain to him may be a severe drain on the ultimate resources of the society. It takes a rather high degree of awareness of the social consequences of procreation before the latency of the Malthusian system can be broken. The fact that it can be broken means, however, that it is not a purely mechanically latent system. If the image of the consequences of the unbridled growth of population is clear in the popular imagination, a society will frequently take steps to insure that it does not reach the Malthusian limit.

The experience of Ireland is an extremely interesting case in point. In the late seventeenth century, the population of Ireland was about two million people living in misery. Then came the seventeenth-century equivalent of Point Four, the introduction of the potato, a technological revolution of first importance enabling the Irish to raise much more food per acre than they had ever done before. The result of this benevolent technological improvement was an increase in population from two million to eight million by 1845. The result of the technological improvement, therefore, was to quadruple the amount of human misery on the unfortunate island. The failure of the potato crop in 1845 led to disastrous consequences. Two million Irish died of starvation; another two million emigrated; and the remaining four million learned a sharp lesson which has still not been forgotten. The population of Ireland has been roughly stationary since that date, in spite of the fact that Ireland is a predominantly Roman Catholic country. The stability has been achieved by an extraordinary increase in the age at marriage.

The Malthusian system is not truly descriptive of the dynamic process. It is rather what the economists call comparative statics. It contemplates, that is to say, an equilibrium state of society; an equilibrium which is determined by certain functions or parameters. If these parameters change, the position of equilibrium likewise changes, and we can discuss the dynamic process as a shift from one equilibrium to the next. This is not, however, a true dynamic process, such as a process exhibiting regular relationships of some sort through time. The Malthusian system says nothing about how long it takes to get from one equilibrium to another or what the path of the transition is likely to be.

There seem to be some true dynamic processes in society, however, which might be described as quasi-latent in character, that is, mechanical models fit them fairly well, and they seem to be fairly independent of the type of image which may overlie them. The effects of technological discoveries can frequently be traced in mechanical systems of this kind. It has been argued, for instance, that the decline of human slavery following the tenth century was a fairly direct result of the invention of the horsecollar which gave Western man, at any rate, a much more effective form of traction than he had ever had before. There is no point in using human slaves for purposes which animal slaves, or still more, mechanical slaves can fulfill more effectively. It has been argued in rather similar vein that the invention of the rudder capable of being set so as to steer a course—an invention which is also attributed to the tenth century—led directly to the geographical expansion of the Western world and the discovery of America. As one school boy put it, "How could Columbus miss it!" Once a ship could go three thousand miles in an approximately straight line, the discovery of America was practically inevitable.

Another chain of latent mechanisms leads from the agricultural changes of the seventeenth century directly to the Industrial Revolution and the expansion of Europe in the past two hundred years. The basic change was the development of root crops and of artificial grasses and clovers. This led to a replacement of the old three-course rotation, or three-field system of the Middle Ages, by the four-course rotation in which the previously fallow field was cleaned of weeds by root crops, and restored in fertility by clover. The result was a substantial change in the output of foodstuffs per acre, particularly of animal feeds. This led to a marked improvement in animal husbandry and livestock breeding. This led to a substantial increase in the output of proteins, both of milk and of meat, and this in turn is unquestionably related to that decline in infant mortality which began about the middle of the eighteenth century in Western Europe, and to which may be attributed almost the whole of the population explosion of the Western world in the past two hundred years. The increasing surplus of foodstuffs from agriculture has permitted the enormous expansion of towns and provided the essential condition for the Industrial Revolution. California today speaks the language of Turnip Townsend, not Junipero Serra.

Part of the development of the image itself may be thought of in terms of these quasi-mechanical models. We have already noticed the idea of a "tree of knowledge"—that is, the regular succession of discovery and invention, which depends on the fact that each inventor stands on the shoulders of those who have gone before him. Each invention, as it occurs, lays the foundation for others. There are only a limited number of possible lines of development.

In spite of the usefulness of these mechanical models, they must be taken with a great deal of reserve. There are very few processes, indeed, in the history of society in which the image does not appear as an important intermediary, if not as the dominating factor. This is true even of the examples we have given of latent processes. The Malthusian process can be modified substantially by an expansion of the image of the procreative process. Technical change itself, as we have already seen, always originates in an image, and it is always propagated by the methods by which images are propagated. If the image is neglected in these processes, it is simply because its influence in simple cases is relatively stable. All the horse-collars in the world did not suffice to abolish slavery until the image of a free society became dominant. In the United States, for instance, it is highly probable that slavery was economically inefficient by the beginning of the nineteenth century, even in the South. The aristocratic image of the Southern gentleman, however, persisted and was even confirmed by his reaction to the agitation of the Northern abolitionists. An image which is about to collapse of its own weight is frequently supported far beyond its time by the efforts of misguided people to push it over. The attacks of the reformers produce defensive mechanisms on the part of the holders of the image. It is identified in the value system with other dearly held values and hence, any messages inconsistent with it are rejected.

Columbus would never have thought to set sail westward had he not had an image of the round world, and a high value in his system for spices. Similarly, the agricultural revolution itself marks the beginning of a period in which change became a welcome element in society instead of a feared and discordant one. The idea of progress always precedes development. In a society in which the image of progress does not exist, even if technological improvements are made accidentally or are made by the mavericks and eccentrics of the society, they will be suppressed and not imitated. In explaining the technological revolution, simple mechanical models are hopelessly inadequate. The conventional explanation that the Industrial Revolution started in England because coal and iron were available turns a conveniently blind eye on the many other places and times in history in which these resources have been equally available and yet nothing has happened. The history of the technological revolution must be written largely in terms of the dynamics of the image- -the image of change as a good and desirable thing introduced by the various religious reformations, and the image of an orderly universe whose secret relations might be explored by experiment and observation. Mechanistic explanations of historical processes are only satisfactory if the intervening images can be neglected as stable. In fact, they can rarely be so neglected, and in explaining why developments take place at one time or in one place and not at another the quasi-independent dynamics of the general image structure of the society must be brought in as an essential element.

Turning now to the more manifest processes in which images play a clear and increasing role, we may distinguish here also between unself-conscious processes in which images play an important role, but in which the process itself is not fully reflected in the images, and conscious processes in which the processes themselves conform to the images of them. The unself-conscious processes in which the image and the process do not always correspond constitute by far the greater part of the processes of society. These exhibit both latent and manifest elements. The purely manifest, completely self-conscious processes are extremely rare, and it may be doubted, indeed, whether any exist in absolutely pure form. No matter how great our fancied understanding of society, no matter how great our presumed sophistication, history always has its surprises for us.

Processes of the mixed or semimanifest type are so common that only a few examples need be given. Their importance lies in the fact that in the course of the processes, the image itself is continually modified by the disappointment and surprises involved in the feedback. Columbus, again, gives a good example. He set sail westward because of an image which was only partly true. He was right in believing that if he went far enough westward, he would reach the Indies. He was wrong in completely underestimating the size of the earth, and in not realizing that a vast unknown continent lay between him and his goal. It is one of the delightful paradoxes of history that Columbus is given credit for the discovery of America. He never realized what he had done. He went to his death apparently still believing that he had found a way to the Indies. The fact that he did not find what he expected to find was a message quite incapable of penetrating the image of the unbroken ocean westward from Spain to the Spice Islands. It was a whole generation before the gradual exploration of the coastlines of the continent and the discovery of great rivers pouring into the Atlantic Ocean made it clear there was indeed a great continent lying between Europe and the East.

An extremely interesting example of a mixed process in which the manifest element is very large is that of the self-justifying image. We have already noticed the phenomenon of self-justifying images in economic life where they are unusually important. Many of the fluctuations of prices in competitive markets, for instance, must be attributed to this phenomenon. If, for instance, there is a general image of an impending rise in the price of some commodity, people will rush to buy it, and this very behavior will bring about the expected rise. In a similar fashion, if there is an expected fall, the rush to sell the commodity will bring it about. In the larger processes of recession and recovery, inflation and deflation, we have already noticed how an image on the part of one person of shall we say an impending depression produces behavior which has the effect of making that depression all the more probable. These phenomena are part of a wider class of processes which might be called chain-reaction processes. Fashion, whether in clothes or ideas, is an interesting example of process. Many of these processes are very imperfectly understood, mainly because we do not know enough about the message system in society and its impact on the images of the fashionable. Some light is thrown on this problem by work which has been done on models of the spread of epidemics. The self-justifying image is also important both in personal and international relations. The man who goes to the world believing that everyone is his enemy will very soon find his suspicions confirmed. The man who acts as if everyone were his friend likewise is likely to be confirmed in his optimism. The same proposition may be made of nations. Both suspicion and trust are, up to a point, self-justifying.

Processes also occur, however, in which images are self-defeating. If all the producers of some commodity share an image of a high price in the future, they will tend to increase their outputs, and as a result of the image of a high price, the future price will in fact be low. Certain very interesting cyclical movements in economic life are related to this type of phenomenon. The hog cycle is perhaps the best known of these, although there are many such. In international relations, the alternation of periods of increasing trust and increasing suspicion likewise point to a curious combination of self-justifying and self-defeating images. Both trust and suspicion justify themselves up to a point, and then are reversed. The problem of how they are reversed, however, is by no means solved.

In tracing the effect of images on the course of history, peculiar attention must be paid to the images of time and especially the images of the future. Curiously enough, it may not be so much the actual content of the image of the future which is important in its effect, but its general quality of optimism or pessimism, certainty or uncertainty, breadth or narrowness. The person or the nation that has a date with destiny goes somewhere, though not usually to the address on the label. The individual or the nation which has no sense of direction in time, no sense of a clear future ahead is likely to be vacillating, uncertain in behavior, and to have a poor chance of surviving.

Those images of the future which are most persistent and which have had the greatest impact on human history seem to be those which are impenetrable to feedback and which maintain themselves by their own internal beauty and consistency. The Jews, for instance, have been maintained as a people through almost unbelievable vicissitudes of history because of their messianic hope and because of their unshakable conviction of being an instrument of God and the great purposes of history. This image, although incapable of confirmation, is reinforced by the reliving of the past in ceremonials of recapitulation. Christianity represents an extension of the Jewish view of the world with the hope of the second coming of Christ replacing the messianic hope of the Jews. Even after two thousand years of disappointment, the adventist hope is still strong enough to create lively sects and subcultures within our own society, and its revival in the church at large is a striking contribution of the ecumenical movement in Protestantism.

The spectacular rise of Islam in its first two centuries is a striking tribute to the creative power of a charismatic image of the future. The fact that the future was in another world was no handicap to the creation of great civilizations in this one. Civilizations based on an essentially charismatic view of the future are, however, unstable. With the almost inevitable fading of the charisma, the dynamic of the culture goes, no matter how great its previous achievements. This seems to be what has happened to Islam in its last five hundred years of history.

One of the most noticeable trends in history has been the rise of manifest images about history itself. Primitive man presumably scratched his way around the world without inquiring much where he had come from or where he was going. The pattern of the seasons imposed on him a certain sense of the regularity of time. But apart from this, one generation was very much like the last. In a very real sense, he had no history. With the coming of writing, agriculture, and the first civilizations, there comes the first great increase in man's time span, and in his sense of time relationships. Here we get the beginnings of ideology, largely at first, in terms of religion. The images of the gods guide man in his destinies, and his destinies may be changed by suitable ceremonies or offerings. This is the pattern, for instance, of the Old Testament. Israel remembers God and is successful and prosperous. Israel forgets God, and is defeated, humiliated, and carried off into captivity. To the modern atheist, inflated with the pride of his own imagined enlightenment, this relational image seems absurd and superstitious. Indeed, as the Hebrew prophets themselves saw clearly, the exact forms of remembrance are unimportant. It is the sacrifice of a contrite heart, not of the flesh of animals, which is true worship. When what might be called the "biblical" image of history is interpreted in these terms, it is seen to be a profound relationship, observable in many different cultures and civilizations in different terms. In the expansive phase of a culture, people are sensitive to the deep, unconscious, latent forces of history and are humble in their presence. In the later stages, they develop pride, the *hubris* of the Greeks, and it is this which brings about their downfall.

All cultures of the past have crystallized and nucleated around their religion because it is the religion which supplies the manifest image of their destiny toward which they feel themselves to be drawn. The dynamics of religion, however, have remained very mysterious. It is clear that the development of religious images follows a certain law and procedure of its own, in many ways independent of change in other parts of society. Attempts to found synthetic religions, for instance, to provide an image structure appropriate to particular political regimes have all ended in miserable failure. When the Roman Empire began to lose faith in its ancient gods, the emperors attempted to substitute emperor-worship. This synthetic religion eventually collapsed before the growing power of Christianity, power which eventually took over the apparatus of the state itself. Similarly, we find in revolutionary France the attempt to erect reason into a religion and to set up festivals of the Goddess of Reason collapsed into absurdity, and the slow organic dynamics of religious change reasserted itself. Even in Russia, where Marxism has provided a quasi-religious ideology with strong formal similarities to Calvinistic Christianity, the state and the party between them have been quite unable either to destroy religion or to provide an acceptable substitute. Indeed, there is some evidence that the Orthodox Church has been purified by persecution and disestablishment, and that as an internal organization, it is stronger than ever it was under the czars. Everywhere in Russia, moreover, there are thriving Baptist communities strong in fellowship and fundamentalist in doctrine. There seems to be a great deal of evidence, therefore, that nonreligious ideologies are incapable of providing the kind of manifest image of life, history, and purpose which are satisfying to the masses of mankind.

There are some who hope for the development of a "true" manifest image of history out of science. Science has given us, they argue, an enormously expanded image of space, time, and relationship and has enormously expanded the powers of man. They hope, therefore, that the next step in science is the expansion of the knowledge and power of man over himself. They look forward to a stage in which all the processes of history become manifest and nothing is latent, nothing is hidden. Carried to its extreme, this would mean in the case of the individual, control over death as well as over disease, and the fulfillment rather than the sacrifice of what the Anglican prayerbook calls "the devices and desires of our own hearts." In the case of society, this view would look forward to the establishment of an unshakable regime of self-conscious social control without war, without revolution, with all conflicts resolvable, and with resources indefinitely conserved. The trouble with all scientific utopias is that once that they are stated, they look remarkably like nightmares—antiseptic visions of a bloodless universe in white, populated by pale immortals.

In the image of history therefore, I plead for humility. I am suspicious of clear manifest images, and of the man with the blueprint. Sophistication in this area usually turns out to be pseudo-sophistication. For what men have thought to be manifest has been continually overturned by the latent.

Let me give an example of what I mean from what seems like the very simple field of the conservation of resources. It is clear to anybody who observes mankind, and especially his economic processes, that human activity, and especially highly technological and civilized activity, is a profound agent of dispersal. In the language of physics, human activity is "entropic." Man inherits concentrated stores of materials—veins of ore, mountains of iron—and the end result of his activity is dispersal of these stores over the face of the earth. Some of them lost in the vast uniformity of the sea, most of them dispersed in innumerable city dumps all over the world. This is a process which obviously cannot go on forever. We look forward to a day in which all the oil has been extracted, all the coal has been mined, all the ore in all the mines has gone, and we think with a slight shudder for our descendants—what then? There are a few processes, it is true, which are at least self-sustaining. Peasant agriculture, sustained yield forestry, cautious fishing. These activities, however, would never sustain a civilization as large and complex as ours. In a very real sense, therefore, man is squandering his great inheritance. His civilization is a flash in the pan in geological time, and we look forward to a future in which small bands of peasant cultivators will gaze awestruck at the ruins of civilization which undermined itself. Here would seem to be an example of a latent process of first magnitude. It is a process, moreover, which would seem to be latent in almost the mechanical sense. No matter how clear our image of it, there is nothing much we can do about it. All that understanding does is to make us thoroughly miserable.

The image is clear, but the future may still surprise us. There are signs, for instance, of anti-entropic processes developing, that is to say, processes which concentrate out of diffuseness rather than diffusing out of the concentrated. The fixation of nitrogen from the air and of magnesium from the sea are cases in point. The discovery of atomic energy has enormously expanded the energy horizon, assuming, that is, that we do not blow ourselves to pieces first.

More than this, the process of the increase of knowledge itself is anti-entropic. It builds structure out of what previously was chaos. It organizes the disorganized. Who can say at this point whether the processes of organization or of disorganization will eventually triumph? To know the answer to this question, one would have to be so wise that to assert the answer would be foolish. By all means let us be as manifest as we can. Let us probe the secrets both of nature and her history, but let us also cultivate a sense of mystery as well as a sense of history. The more we know, the more we know that we don't know. The searchlight of the manifest makes more apparent the darkness of the latent beyond it. What this means in practice is that our response should be always to an uncertain image. We should not put all our eggs in the basket that happens to be around at the moment. In the jargon of the economist, our image of history should never be so free from uncertainty that we feel we can afford to dispense with liquid assets.

9

Subcultures and the Subuniverses of Discourse

WE HAVE OBSERVED
that although the image of an individual person is subjective in the sense that it is a property or structure of his own organization, it is not necessarily "private" in the sense that it is unrelated to other images. We have already developed the concept of a "public image," which consists of the shared images of many individuals. We must now take cognizance of the observation, however, that there is not a single public image, but there are many public images, as many indeed as there are cultures and subcultures within the great frame of the human race.

A public image is a product of a universe of discourse, that is, a process of sharing messages and experiences. The shared messages which build up the public image come both from nature and from other men. A group of people talking around the table do not each receive the same messages. Indeed, each perceives the situation from his own position. Nevertheless, the image of the situation which is built up in each of the individuals is highly similar, at least in regard to the spatial and temporal image. In a group of close friends the personal and relational images may also be very similar. In a group of hostile or indifferent people they may not be. The symbolic images which come, for instance, in speech from other individuals also play an important part in building up the public image. There is a famous experiment in social psychology in which each individual in a group of people is asked to express his perception of some simple physical difference, for instance, whether one line is longer than another. All but one of the individuals in the group are instructed to make a "false response." They are to state firmly that in their perception *a* is larger than *b*, when in "fact" the reverse is the case. In many cases the victim of the experiment (the man who does not read the *Philadelphia Bulletin*) is rapidly persuaded to disbelieve the messages of his senses by the symbolic messages from his peers.

A subculture may be defined as a group of people sharing a public image. This need not be a conscious image, and the group need not be conscious that they are sharing it. If, however, there are basic similarities in the images of the different individuals in the group, the behavior of the group will reflect and will, in general, reinforce the similarities. This is because the symbolic messages which are issued from individuals in the group reflect in some degree the image which they possess, and these messages when received by other individuals in the group confirm the image which is held by the recipient.

One of the very interesting problems in the study of the image and one which is still largely unsolved is that of the conditions under which images of different individuals converge under the impact of symbolic communication and the conditions under which they diverge. One may venture the hypothesis that there is some degree of similarity among the images of a group of interacting people which forms, as it were, a critical watershed. If the images are more similar than this critical degree of similarity they will converge under the stimulus of intercourse. If the images are less similar than this critical degree of similarity, they will diverge under the same set of stimuli. Suppose, for instance, that we have a group of people who are sitting around gossiping about another person who is known to all of them. Let us suppose that they all begin the conversation with a somewhat unfavorable image of the person under discussion. The images will be somewhat different because of the different experiences of the individuals: some may have a fairly favorable image, some very unfavorable. As the conversation proceeds, these images are likely to converge, and alas, are likely to converge in the unfavorable direction. Suppose, however, there are one or two people in the group who hold strongly differing images from the rest of the group, suppose, for instance, that they think the person under discussion is an extremely fine person. Under the stimulus of the conversation, the group may break up into two subgroups—each with a convergent image of its own. Or, of course, the minority may win over the majority, or may be won over to the majority. Cases could undoubtedly be found, for instance, in which an initial jury vote of eleven to one against a defendant eventually became a unanimous vote in his favor, or in which the initial dissidents were won over, or in which the jury became more hopelessly split as discussion proceeded. Changes in the image as a result of symbolic intercourse would depend, of course, on the skill of the communicators as well as on the initial situation. The whole art of persuasion is the art of perceiving the weak spots in the images of others and of prying them apart with well-constructed symbolic messages.

The more complex the society, the more likely are we to find individuals possessing many roles and sharing in

134

many different subcultures and universes of discourse. A man may share one image with his colleagues at work, another with his wife and family at home, another with his political party members, yet another with his co-religionists. Interesting problems arise when the images in these different roles are inconsistent. Many of the personality difficulties in a complex society may be attributed to this inconsistency in the public image in the various roles in which a single individual participates. The businessman who is expected to be keen, sharp, and competitive in the office, is expected to be loving and co-operative at home; the young man is taught love in the church and hate in the army; the repressed hatreds of our childhood roles pursue us like furies to the analyst's couch in later years.

Let us consider briefly some of the subcultures of our own society with the public images which they help to create, and which support them. We have first the standard intellectual subcultures of universities. In medieval times, the university subculture was dominated by philosophy and theology. Today it is dominated by science. It enjoys a complex public image widely shared but characterized by specialization. There is a shared image built up for instance from the astronomers' and geographers' views of space, the geologists' views of time, physical, chemical and biological notions of relationship, and so on. Because of the high degree of specialization however, each specialist sees the image, as it were, from his own vantage point. The image of his own specialty he sees in great detail, related specializations he sees somewhat more vaguely, and distant fields sometimes he hardly perceives at all. There is remarkable ignorance of the social sciences for instance among natural scientists, and a similar ignorance of natural science among the social scientists. It can hardly be said, therefore, that there is a single public image uniting the intellectual subculture. Rather there is a series of departmental and specialized images which form some kind of an overlapping continuum.

There is perhaps more uniformity in the value images of the intellectual subculture than there is in the other parts of the image. Skill in symbolic interaction is highly valued, whether in writing or in speech. Large body movements are valued negatively; intellectuals do not slap each other on the back, indulge in horseplay, or punch each other in the nose. Small and subtle body movements are highly valued—the subtle gesture, the sincere handshake, the intelligent laugh. Humor is highly valued—so much so that it becomes a highly serious matter. Almost the worst thing that one can say about an intellectual is that he has no sense of humor. Humor, however, is strictly reserved for private conversation and social intercourse. In public expressions and especially in scientific writings, high value is placed on dullness, obscurity, and the lack of wit. High value is placed, oddly enough, both on impersonality and on warmth in personal relationship. The latter is perhaps only true in American universities where people are expected to be friendly, to call each other by their first names, and to think as well of each other as possible. In European universities, the reverse is the case. High values are placed on intolerance, disagreeableness, and snobbery. In the world of science, it is a conventional value that the scientist is objectively and impersonally in pursuit of truth. This image is not always confirmed by the feedback. Nevertheless, it is a powerful image, and it makes intellectuals more willing to accept criticism and modification of their views than would otherwise be the case. Each discipline or department within the general subculture tends to develop rituals and value systems of its own. In American universities, elaborate apparatus is highly valued—the cyclotron, the electronic calculator. The collection of data, that is, of the transcribed results of scientific activity is also highly valued. Theory tends to be valued for the social prestige attached to incomprehensibility rather than for its relevance to the activities which are actually carried on.

The division of the intellectual subuniverse of discourse into sub-subuniverses or departments of discourse has become a serious problem in our time. To some extent it is a result simply of the increasing size of the transcribed image of the intellectual universe which makes it impossible for any single individual to become familiar with it all. Furthermore, the departmental organization of the universities means that an individual can satisfy his need for gregariousness within the confines of his own department of specialization. We find, therefore, that the lines of symbolic communication fall almost wholly within departments, and very rarely extend from one department to another. The more this happens, however, the harder it becomes to break through the departmental barriers, because each department develops not only an image of its own but also a language of its own. It is not merely that there are technical terms to be learned, but the same word is used in a different sense in different fields of study, and it is necessary to unlearn the use in one's own field before one can understand others.

A problem has been created for the unity of the public image in the intellectual world by the enormous development of mathematics and its increasing use in the sciences. In one sense it can be said that mathematics is a language, although it is not a complete language. It is perhaps best regarded as a shorthand rather than as a language, that is, it is a very convenient way of expressing in a short form what would otherwise take an intolerable amount of long-windedness. It is also not a universal language. It cannot be used for talking about everything, but only about certain things. It is a jargon rather than a language. Nevertheless, it is an enormously useful and powerful jargon, and its development has been abundantly justified by its results. It presents, however, a real problem for communication. In the first place, it is more difficult to translate results from mathematics into English or any standard language than it is to convert standard languages to each other. The intellectual who cannot read, let us say, German is at some slight disadvantage if his native language is English. There are some important works in German which may be relevant to his interests which are not translated. Something also is always lost in translation, especially the more subtle nuances and flavors of the language. Goethe's *Faust*, for instance, which is a profound and moving poem in its original tongue, is an unspeakable bore in translation. Nevertheless, the loss is a small one and can be borne. Ignorance of foreign languages especially on the part of those who are fortunate enough to have been brought up in one of the great world languages is an inconvenience, it is no more. Ignorance of mathematics, however, is a dark shade thrown across many windows of the intellectual universe. Not only is it difficult to translate works out of mathematics into ordinary language, there is very little incentive to do so. Of all specialists, mathematicians are the proudest and the most governed by esthetic and nonrational considerations. They hate to have the refined beauties of their symbolism debased by the earthy dross of common speech. Their attitude is reminiscent of the English-speaking residents of Montreal who dismiss the language problem with the reflection that after all everybody learns to speak English sooner or later.

I began this section by attempting to describe, in very rough outline, the public image of the intellectual world. Like Antony, I seem to have come to bury it rather than to praise it. Even on the vital matter of intellectual freedom, the image of the academic world is split and divided. We do not know from whence comes our peace or our prosperity. The universe of discourse is crumbling into a multiverse, and in one's more depressed moments one looks forward to a time when the progress of science will grind to a standstill in a morass of mutual incomprehensibility. Out of our intellectual pride, we may be building a new Tower of Babel.

The picture is not entirely without hope. As on many occasions in the development of mankind, awareness of a problem results in measures taken for a solution. In recent years, there has been an increasing interest in interdisciplinary and interdepartmental communication. This has almost reached the dimensions of what might be called an interdisciplinary movement. There are small groups of people here and there interested in the unity of science, in general systems theory, etc. The present work itself is an attempt to show throughout the multitudinous diversity of the academic world a certain single thread which runs through many disciplines in the concept of the image. I myself have not given up the hope that the convergence of theoretical systems in the various disciplines may yet produce something like a general theory, a set of concepts, relationships, and references which can provide, as it were, skeletons for the unified public image of the intellectual world. We shall be deluding ourselves, however, if we think either that we have this or even that it is in sight. We may look forward to such a unification with hope, but by no means with certainty.

Closely allied, and in many ways overlapping with the intellectual subculture, are the professional subcultures. Many of these have one foot, as it were, in the universities through the professional schools: medicine, law, engineering, architecture, education, social work, etc. Insofar as the products of these schools do not, in general, stay in the universities, but disperse into the society at large to practice the professional skills which they have acquired, they develop a culture of their own and an image of their own. Professional subcultures merge almost imperceptibly into occupational subcultures in general. Wherever there is shoptalk there is an occupational subculture. The doctor, the lawyer, the tinker, the tailor, the plumber, the painter, the soldier, the sailor, even the beggarman and the thief all have their own jargon, their specialized means of communication, their own discourse, and their own public images. The sociology of the professions and specialized occupations is a fascinating field in which a good deal of work has been done. Much remains to be done, however, in studying the way in which the public image of the occupation and its public value system is built up in the minds both of the neophytes and of the practitioners.

Difficulties arise because of the economic principle that the prosperity of any specialized occupation depends upon its ability to keep people out of it. There has been a strong tendency to set up artificial barriers to communication among the trades and professions. The medieval concept of a craft as a "mystery," a body of knowledge and skill wholly inaccessible to those outside it, and only open to the initiates allowed in by the grace of the present practitioners is an idea that dies hard. Every profession and craft which has a self-conscious image of itself in the minds of its members is to some extent a conspiracy against the public. This is the shady side of "professional ethics." The three basic principles of professional ethics are: (1) strict sanctions against price cutting in any form; (2) strict regulation of entry into the profession; (3) a tacit agreement to cover up the mistakes of the practitioners by a conspiracy of silence directed toward preventing any feedback to the public. As a counterweight one may concede a measure of standardization of the professional product and some protection of the consumer.

Fortunately for the progress of mankind, monopolies of knowledge are notoriously unstable. Craft mysteries are continuously being made obsolete by the rise of new crafts and new techniques. Even the dignified professions are continually being challenged by new professions and substitute specializations. The frock-coated monopoly of the doctors for instance in the nineteenth century was sharply challenged by the rise of osteopathy, chiropractic, and even Christian Science. Health is a funny business. The soul-saving monopoly of the church was broken by the rise of Protestantism and denominationalism. Even the universities are challenged by correspondence schools, business institutes, and the educational programs of corporations. What this means is that where the rigidities of a professional subculture do not allow the image of its practitioners to change rapidly enough, new images will arise, outside the profession or the established subculture, and create professions and subcultures of their own.

Religious subcultures and the images which correspond to them are of great interest and importance in the understanding of the general social process. They are particularly difficult to study, however, and have not received the attention they deserve, partly because of the difficulty of identifying or describing the image which characterizes them. The "official image" of the church or sect as embodied in its creeds, sacred books, rituals, and official pronouncements is usually only a part of the image of the members and participants. Indeed, there is a strong tendency for the formal image to diverge sharply from the informal image in the course of time, the formal image being much more stable than the informal image. We see a good example of this in the extraordinary cultural and even religious diversity within the Roman Catholic Church. Because of the hierarchical structure of the church, all Catholic churches of the Latin rite everywhere have the same official image, the same creed, the same canon, the same ritual, even the same official language—Latin. Even to the most casual observer, however, it is clear that the Catholic Church in different parts of the world represents a quite astonishing diversity, not only of social structure, but even of religious experience and images. The Catholic Church in the United States, for instance, is much more like a Protestant "denomination" than the austere, dominant, and rather terrifying church in Spain or even of Quebec. National characteristics impose themselves on the Church. In the highlands of Peru, the Church may be little more than a thin veneer on a pre-Christian culture. In Poland and in Ireland, it is the repository of generations of nationalistic agitation and of fierce memories of repression. In Quebec, it is the agency for the maintenance of an old preindustrial culture against the inroads of English-speaking vulgarity.

The sociology and psychology of religion are one thing, however. Religion is another. The image of the subcultures include many things which are not specifically religious. The church performs many of the functions of the club, the lodge, the marriage market, and the clinical psychologist. All these things are included in the image, but they can be taken out, and something still remains. What remains is religious experience as such. It is customary among scientists, even among social scientists, to regard the religious experience as such as essentially private, ineffable, incommunicable, and therefore almost by definition suspect. It is difficult to maintain this position, however, in the face of the enormous literature of the spiritual life, a literature which is the transcript of a universe of discourse, at least as public as any other. When the mystic says his experience cannot be described, he is in fact describing it. Millions of good Methodists have known perfectly well what John Wesley meant when he said that his heart was "strangely warmed." There is here a universe of discourse in which St. Augustine and George Fox speak to each other across the centuries, and in which the Christian mystic and the Sufi can alike exchange confidences.

In addition to these more intellectual subcultures in which images tend to be verbalized and recorded in the form of transcripts, there are innumerable folk or class subcultures in which the image is not perhaps as well verbalized or symbolized, but in which it is no less public or real. It is not only the primitive people studied by anthropologists that can be said to have cultures of their own. Within any complex societies, there are groups more or less isolated from the rest of the community which develop public images which they share within the group, but do not share with outsiders. From the street corner to the executive suite, our own society is honeycombed by these subcultures. The image around which they are organized is not so much a spatial, temporal, or relational image; these images they tend to share with the world around them. It is rather a value image. This value image is frequently summarized in the form of an ideal type or personality. Among criminals there are ideal types of successful operators, people who "get away with it" in the unceasing warfare between the individual and the society around him. In street corner society, again there is an ideal image of the successful person, the "champ" whose physical prowess elevates him to a position of leadership in a society with such a value system. In the culture of the factory, the ideal type is the "good Joe," friendly, expansive, generous, no rate-buster, highly skilled but content to use his skill in moderation. In the executive suite, the ideal type is written in terms of the efficient, keen, and plausible man of distinction.

We need to know much more about the generation of these images of the ideal personality. There can be little doubt that they arise in part from embodiment of the ideal in the form of a dominating or charismatic individual. The persistence of the ideal, however, often in the absence of any official or written transcript of it, is a striking phenomenon, and there are many interesting problems related to how these ideals change, originate, and compete with one another. The phenomenon of social mobility can hardly be understood except in terms of the competition of ideal types. What is it, for instance, that drives an ambitious boy from the poolroom to the night school or to the university? What is it also that leads the sons of the elite back to the poolroom or its more expensive equivalents in Reno? Like the gods and goddesses of ancient mythology one sometimes almost gets the impression of ideal types battling above the clouds for the minds and allegiances of men. Sometimes the gods fall down from Olympus quite suddenly and without explanation. The "pukka sahib" fell from Olympus in the moment of Kipling's apotheosis of him, and where is he now? It is the fall of the ideal image that leads to the collapse of empires and the decay of cultures, yet how little we know about the forces which support or destroy these powerful beings.

Within the protecting walls of the subcultures which they themselves have built, the images grow, change, develop, and decay almost with a life of their own. Each discipline of the academic world follows its own line of development, often without much regard to what is happening in other disciplines, or even in the world outside. Because its lines of communication all turn inward, the members of the subculture devote themselves to the elaborate solution of problems which they themselves create. In Catholic theology, for instance, we see an image of an intervening and incarnate father-god elaborating itself within the protecting walls of the Church till it produces the doctrines of infallibility of the Pope and the Assumption of the Virgin. The elevation of Jesus almost out of the sight of the faithful leads almost inevitably to the worship of Mary, and the image of the Virgin, as Henry Adams has so beautifully described, built the cathedrals of Europe. In Protestantism, a rediscovery of the immediacy of religious experience and the joyful recapturing of the Divine Immanence develops also under pressure of the environment into a vulgarization of divinity and the acceptance of God as a business partner. In economics an initial misconception of the nature of the pricing process produces the labor theory of value, Karl Marx, and a monstrous theology of value. Chemistry had its phlogiston, and even biology has its Lysenko.

One may venture on the proposition that any tendency toward the breakdown of the isolation of subcultures is likely to lead to rapid change in them. As long as a subculture is isolated from the rest of the world, with all its lines of communication lying within, its image tends to be self-supporting and self-perpetuating. All the messages which are received by the individuals participating confirm the images which they have, because to a large extent the messages originate in these images. A mutual admiration society is a fine way of persuading us that we are all fine fellows for nobody ever contradicts us. Once, however, the barriers which divide subcultures are broken, messages are received from other subcultures which are inconsistent with the images held in one. The reaction to this situation is either rapid re-establishment of the barriers between the subcultures or it is a rapid change in the images of all of them. The extraordinary rapidity with which images have changed in the last two hundred years is perhaps mainly a result of increased communication among previously isolated subcultures. It is easy to overestimate, however, the extent of this breakdown of isolation. As we have seen, in the intellectual subculture, isolation actually seems to be increasing because of the development of specialization and the compartmentalization of language. Communication between the intellectual and the religious subcultures is precarious in the extreme. It depends almost entirely on the doubtful abilities of a few individuals who participate in both. Society owes an enormous debt to those marginal men who live uneasily in two different universes of discourse. Society is apt to repay this debt by making them thoroughly uncomfortable and still more marginal.

The breakdown of physical isolation still remains one of the dominant features of the history of images in the past few hundred years. The transformation of Japan in the nineteenth century is a striking example of the effect of such physical communication. The coming of communism to China represents an even more striking example. Like Christianity and Islam, communism is a faith and an image of society in history which has deep roots in eschatological Judaism. Looked at in the long view of history, the present events in China may represent not so much the contact of the Chinese with Marx, as their contact with Moses.

We must not always assume, of course, that images are strongest in isolation and that contact with other subcultures always breaks them down. A limited amount of contact with other subcultures frequently reinforces a value system. This is particularly true wherever the value system is conceived in somewhat negative terms, where we have a "not-image" rather than an image. An excellent example of a not-image is anticommunism or anticapitalism. The clear image here is that of the enemy or the other, not of the self. Under these circumstances the messages from the other image actually reinforce the not-image. Increased communication up to a point leads to reinforcement of the separate images and not to their destruction. Images, both of social class and of nationality, are sufficiently often of this type to make one hesitate before recommending a universal program of getting people together in the interests of brotherly love. Occasionally, the way to keep people together is to keep them apart. The British Commonwealth is an interesting example of a society united by distances large enough to overcome mutual dislike.

10

Eiconics; A New Science?

I HAVE NOW PURSUED
the concept of the image through a number of different
fields in hasty and summary fashion. It has been my hope
to be suggestive rather than exhaustive and to open up
some new vistas rather than to complete a picture. I hope,
nevertheless, that I have been able to indicate that in the
concept of a message-image relationship there is a conceptual and theoretical scheme of remarkable unifying
power. It is one important thread that seems to run
through a number of different disciplines and sciences.
In this chapter I want to raise the question partly in jest
but partly also in seriousness whether the concept of the
image cannot become the abstract foundation of a new
science, or at least a cross-disciplinary specialization. As
I am indulging in the symbolic communication of an
image of images I will even venture to give the "science"
a name—Eiconics—hoping thereby to endow it in the
minds of my readers with some of the prestige of classical antiquity. I run some risk perhaps of having my new
science confused with the study of icons. A little confusion, however, and the subtle overtones of half-re-
membered associations are all part of the magic of the
name.

Anyone who has the audacity, indeed the foolhardiness, to proclaim the establishment of a new science must be prepared either to withstand heavy criticism or at least to disarm it by suitable disclaimers. Let me first of all then play the devil's advocate against myself and consider how far in the words of the most devastating book review ever written, "What is new is not good and what is good is not new." My new science like every other new thing is not particularly new. Like every neonate it comes into the world after a period of gestation, and it comes burdened with a large genetic heritage. So multisexual is the reproduction of images, furthermore, that it comes not with the pedigree of two parents alone, but with many. My new image is no exception to the law of the generation of images. It arises partly out of the innumerable messages which have come to me both from the transcript of our society, the books and the papers—all too few alas —which I have read, and also from face-to-face conversations with many individuals. Unfortunately, I find it easier to remember messages than their sources. The bills of lading and the accounts of my fine new temple of the mind are in shocking disorder.

I must make some attempt, however, to trace what is not new in the new science. I will begin with economics, which is the field I know best and which, alas, I must confess, has contributed least. The tradition of economics is pretty sharply anti-eiconical and mechanistic—from Adam Smith to Pareto it has been celestial mechanics applied to earthly things. Even in the theory of economic behavior, as we have seen, the problem of information and knowledge has been strangely neglected. I am familiar with only two—completely unrelated—pieces of work in economics which make any serious attempt to contribute to this problem. The first is an essay by F. W. Hayek, the second is the work of the economic psychologist, George Katona. To these men I offer—whether they accept it or not—the honor of being the first eiconists in their field.

Eiconics has somewhat deeper roots in sociology, especially in the sociology of knowledge. The sociology of knowledge itself has a curious history. It originates either as a favorable or as an unfavorable reaction to the Marxian interpretation of history. Marx did not, as some later psychologists have tried to do, deny the existence of an image. He was concerned, however, with showing that the history of ideas was a sort of caboose attached to the great steam engine of technological development and class struggle. People think what they do, according to Marx, because of their position in the structure of society. Marx had to recognize himself, unfortunately, as an exception to this universal rule. This is always one of the difficulties of a sociology of knowledge. If one is too successful in explaining why people think what they do in terms of factors and forces lying outside the ideational structure, this is apt to destroy the validity of the theory itself, because the views of the sociologist of knowledge are determined by sociology. He is always in the position of having to assert that nobody is queer except himself.

The two names principally associated with the sociology of knowledge in Germany are Max Scheler, who used it to beat down the pretensions of the positivists from an essentially conservative Catholic viewpoint, and Karl Mannheim, who used it to try and make an honest woman out of the Marxist interpretation of history. The sociology of knowledge then became a refugee from Germany along with a number of other distinguished ideas and settled down at the University of Chicago, where to the best of my knowledge, it has been living quietly ever since. Unfortunately, the English language is not so well adapted as the German for saying nothing in particular about things in general. This has perhaps hampered the development of the more philosophical aspects of the theory in this country.

Psychology started out with an image of the mind as a sort of jigsaw puzzle of ideas. The science took a firmly anti-eiconical turn, however, with the development of behaviorism. It is a little difficult to believe that Dr. Watson actually believed what he is supposed to have believed, namely, that Dr. Watson was an epiphenomenon. It is, however, in the record that this is what psychologists used to believe. The attempt to interpret the organism as a stimulus-response slot machine was terribly good for the rat business, but it certainly was not eiconics. With the coming of the Gestalt school, however, psychology began to take a sharply eiconical direction. Psychologists began to conceive the organism not merely as a jigsaw puzzle or as a slot machine but as an organization. The so-called "new look" in perception theory is an even more significant turn in the direction of eiconics. Far from being the uninhibited and direct impressions which they were once supposed to be, sense perceptions are now revealed to be clever little fellows well trained in the hard school of experience and only admitted to the organism after passing a severe test in value theory.

Social psychology has been eiconical almost from the start. It may be indeed that George Mead will have to be given the credit for being the first eiconist. He has the concept of the image firmly in mind although he does not perceive, I think, the breadth and generality of the concept in the nonhuman universe. The field theory of Kurt Lewin and his group dynamics school is also a clear example of the use of the image in social-psychological theories. The idea of behavior as "locomotion" toward the most highly valued part of the field of the image is due to this school.

Anthropology has only recently become interested in the image. It passed through a long stage (no doubt necessarily) when it was mainly concerned with the accumulation of descriptions of artifacts and observable behavior. Its most recent developments, however, point firmly in the direction of eiconics. The work of Clyde Kluckhohn and the Harvard group is particularly important in this connection, especially their studies of values. The doctrine of cultural relativism developed among anthropologists, partly as a mere protest against the cultural imperialism of their own Western society. Most anthropologists of this period give the impression of being refugees from a mission station. One can hardly be concerned with pointing out the relativity of various value systems, however, without being concerned to study them, and this lands the anthropologist firmly in eiconics.

A few philosophically minded biologists and physicists also seem to have been moving in this direction. The fascinating suggestions of Schroedinger regarding the relation of entropy to life, the work of Bertalanffy on open systems theory and of Ager on the relation of perception to behavior in the lower organisms all point in an eiconical direction. The beginning of this movement in biology may perhaps be traced to the pioneering work of Jennings on the behavior of the lower animals.

The most eiconical of all the "official" disciplines is, of course, psychoanalysis. It is, indeed, almost the whole business of the psychoanalyst to explore the image, both conscious and unconscious, and his therapeutic method depends largely on the theory that the subconscious should be brought into consciousness. By so doing he helps to modify the image by permitting its suppressed parts to develop according to its own internal laws in a way that will restore the patient to mental health. Without an organic theory of knowledge the work of Freud is completely incomprehensible. In the work of some later heretics, such as Jung, the psychoanalytic school seems to be going too far in the direction of awarding images a status which is almost independent of the organism that supports them and that creates them.

In the development of my own thinking in this direction I must confess that it has not been the contribution of the official disciplines which has influenced me most. The three works which have most influenced me in this direction and which seem to me to have contributed the most toward the establishment of a science of eiconics all lie outside the regular academic disciplines. They are first, the pioneering work of Chester Barnard, *The Functions of the Executive*. From this comes the central idea of the executive or "central agent" of any organization as a receiver of information and an issuer of orders. The second work is Norbert Wiener's *Cybernetics*. In this the notion of the executive as the center of a control mechanism whereby through the feedback of information divergences from ideal values are corrected, fills out and supplements the theory of organization of Barnard. The third book, Shannon and Weaver's *The Mathematical Theory of Communication*, is the bible of "information theory." The development of a mathematical concept of information parallels in its importance the development of the concepts of mass and energy in physics. It has opened up the possibility of a new and more quantitative approach to the whole problem of organization.

In very rough outline and with many omissions, these

are the building blocks. The question is do they build a discipline, that is, an image that is capable of organizing a whole field of intellectual activity. Is the image of the image capable of developing researchable hypotheses, testable propositions, and of producing an orderly growth of theoretical insights? At this stage one cannot give a categorical answer to this question. Only the future will tell. It is possible, however, to formulate some of the hopes and fears, some of the possibilities, and some of the objections which surround the new infant.

Let me admit first that the theoretical structure which I have outlined in these pages is by no means complete and that it has some real weaknesses.

It is true that information theory has introduced an element of sharpness of focus into the concept of the organizational process and the formation of images which was not there before and which constitutes the real difference perhaps, between the type of theory I have been proposing and the earlier work, let us say, of George Mead. Nevertheless, information theory as it stands today is by no means adequate to bear the burden of providing the necessary abstractions. The information concept of Shannon is merely a statistic, descriptive of a distribution, like, let us say, the standard deviation. It is not a measure of any mysterious or impalpable quality of a message. It is not even the same concept as that of entropy, although its mathematical form is the same. It is a convenient statistic for use in certain problems in solving the communication of messages over limited channels. In and of itself it is no more than this. It is, of course, a most suggestive concept and it suggests analogies and mechanisms far beyond its actual limited sphere of proved usefulness. Suggestion, however, is not realization, and it must be admitted that the information concept as we have it at present is confined to an extremely limited level of abstraction. It is still quite incapable, for instance, of dealing with semantic content. Information in the Shannon sense is simply "an improbable arrangement." It is a measure of the departure from chaos or randomness. It does not tell us anything about the direction in which that departure takes place. There are a great many dimensions of the message, in other words, which cannot be accounted for by information theory as we have it today. The problem of reducing these dimensions to appropriate abstract concepts, however, is an extremely difficult one, and we cannot pretend that it has been solved. It may well be that the future usefulness of the new discipline is going to depend on the solution, at least at some levels, of this problem of semantic content. It is one thing to say that an image has a structure and that this structure is affected in various ways by the messages which impinge on it. It is quite another thing to be able to abstract from this structure those characteristics which are essential to the problem in hand.

Although much needs to be done in the direction of putting content, even mathematical content, into the theory of the image, nevertheless, the fact that in a sense we can perceive what needs to be done is encouraging. It may be that like Moses I have only brought the reader to Nebo, from which tantalizing glimpses of a promised land may be obtained. Like Moses, also (and let the comparison stop there), I am pretty sure that I shall not go over Jordan. Some Joshua must arise if the promised land is to be taken. But I must confess I cannot avoid the impression that the theory of the image as I have outlined it is, indeed, a point from which a promised land may be seen.

Let me now take up the question of the potentialities

of the theory of the image in organizing empirical research. Is there here a level of abstraction from which the universe may be surveyed and according to which important segments of the universe can be organized? If there is, then in spite of the limitations of the theory itself it has some claim to be a symbol of a new discipline. Is there here in the theory of the image, a new language in which researchers in what now seem to be many different fields can communicate easily and pool their results? Is there—what is even more important—in the theory of the image an organizing principle which will permit an orderly development of the theoretical image itself as a result of the feedbacks from empirical research?

I am prepared to argue that at least in the social sciences a great deal of the empirical research that goes on today is in fact directed toward the image of the image. This research is scattered over many different fields, and for this reason the results are often not communicated among the researchers, and hence a good deal of effort is wasted through this lack of communication. Once the matter is presented to them a great many empirical social scientists may discover that they have been practicing eiconical research all the time, as Molière's Monsieur Jourdain discovered to his immense satisfaction that he had been speaking prose all his life.

Let me suggest areas, therefore, in which eiconical research is going on. The first area which comes to mind is, of course, psychoanalysis. Unfortunately, the clinical nature of the observations and records of this discipline present a serious handicap to the development of its theoretical system. By the very nature of his profession, the psychoanalyst can divulge the revelations of his patient only in the most general form or only after the participants are no longer interested. In spite of this handicap (which is perhaps more severe in this occupation than it is even in the profession of medicine generally) a certain amount of generalized feedback from the experience of psychoanalysts toward the general image of psychoanalytic theory does take place. Psychoanalysis, however, suffers under another very severe handicap from the point of view of empirical feedback. Because of its clinical nature the sample of the total universe of images which it investigates is of necessity extremely biased. The bulk of psychoanalytic data comes from pathological cases, that is, from people whose images are in some sense troublesome. The people who go to psychoanalysts are an extremely unrepresentative sample of the population, both as to income level, as to family history, and as to general characteristics. Some foundation might consider the possibility of supporting the psychoanalysis of a carefully stratified sample of the population to gain some idea of the extent of the distortion of the psychoanalytic image which is introduced by the nature of its sample. What is important here, however, is not so much the deficiencies in the empirical material in psychoanalysis as the fact that this empirical material exists and develops. If anyone believes that images are wholly inaccessible to inquiry he must denounce psychoanalysis as pure charlatanry. Charlatanry there may be; but it is not pure charlatanry, and in that fact lies the hope for vigorous empirical research even on the subconscious image.

Another important area of research in the social sciences which is primarily concerned with research into the image is public opinion polling. One can admit all the deficiencies in the method, and at the same time one has to confess that there is an important residue of results. The problem of eliciting information about images by the simple device of recording answers to questions is by no means insoluble. We do not necessarily have to take these answers at face value. There are difficult and subtle problems of interpretation, and I think one would have to admit there is a certain absence of theoretical structure. Nevertheless, even with the crude apparatus which we have today the results are impressive. They are particularly impressive because wherever the polling is done regularly and with some systematic notion in mind we can perceive not only something about the nature of the image but also how it changes. It is by no means impossible by the method to trace the development of a public image. To take but a single example, the long series that we now have on the image of the American public toward World War II is of extraordinary interest in interpreting the development of the public image in this period under the impact of different messages. The theory of the formation of the image, even in the rather vague form in which I left it, would be of great usefulness in organizing this material.

The work of the Survey Research Center of the University of Michigan is an even more striking example of investigation into images by methods which are more rigorous than those of the commercial public opinion pollsters. In the survey of consumer finances, for instance, we have a careful and long-continued inquiry into the image of the consumer, especially in regard to the future. Here again it is the cumulative impact of these data which is important rather than the results of any particular survey. As we trace the dynamics of consumer intentions through time, we have again a magnificent opportunity to study the impact of messages upon the image. Here again, the theory of image formation would seem to be an essential theoretical construct to guide this great empirical work.

Another important area of empirical research in which the notion of the image is of great importance is that of social psychology, especially research into small groups and into communication networks and their effects. The concept of the image as a field of potential behavior is quite fundamental to group dynamics, as we have already noticed. Much research these days in industrial sociology and psychology is directed toward exploring the nature of the image of the work environment possessed by individuals in different roles, and the way in which experience modifies this image. Here again, there is reason for believing that the theory of the image is a basic part of any empirical work in this general area.

I cannot speak with any direct knowledge of empirical research in biology. Nevertheless, there are indications that the kind of conceptual framework which I have been outlining is becoming of increasing importance in this field. The work of Quastler on the application of information theory to biological problems is a case in point. Information theory, itself, has not perhaps been quite as fruitful in these applications as was originally expected. I throw out the challenge to the biologist whether the introduction of the concept of the image is not what is needed to make information theory take its proper place in the interpretation of the behavior of organisms.

Let me recapitulate by stating the problem in the language of my own theory. Is it possible to create organized feedbacks within the general framework of the scientific subculture which will alter the public image of images of this subculture in useful, creative, and organically growing ways? From what I have said above, it is clear that this process is already going on. The answer to the above question, therefore, must be yes. The real question at issue is, perhaps, whether the process will be improved by being made more self-conscious. Will the eiconists do any better for realizing that they are eiconists? I think a tentative affirmative can also be given to this question. The present isolation of the workers in many different disciplines who are actually co-operating in the same field can hardly be defended.

I have been arguing that the theory of the image does provide a basis for the integration for a great deal of intellectual work which previously has seemed rather unrelated. I am arguing, that is to say, that eiconics deserves recognition as a new discipline. Does this mean that it is a new science? In order to answer this question, we must examine briefly the process by which sciences originate and departments of study are established.

In the history of the development of the sciences and the departments of the academic world, it is fairly clear that the most usual means of the establishment of a new department of knowledge is by a process akin to cell division. The new department originates within the confines of an old department. It grows as a subdivision of the old department until it reaches the stage at which it feels strong enough to branch out into a department of its own. There are undoubtedly important exceptions to this rule, especially in the case of disciplines which have originated in two departments simultaneously. Chemistry grew within the general confines of "natural philosophy," which gradually divided into physics on the one side and chemistry on the other. Sociology generally begins as the subdivision of a department of economics. Economics, itself, originated under the protection of moral philosophy. It would not be difficult to trace a type of a genetic tree of the sciences, all of them in a sense branching out from philosophy. As we move toward the present day we find more examples of sciences produced by sexual union rather than by parthenogenesis. In the natural sciences, physical chemistry owes perhaps more to chemistry than it does to physics, historically; nevertheless, it represents a real union between the two. Biochemistry and biophysics likewise represent sexual generation of a discipline. In the social sciences, social psychology also betrays its double origin: a hyphenated name is a sure mark of distinguished but double ancestry.

We now seem to be entering a period in which the development of new disciplines is taking a new turn. Instead of a new discipline developing quietly within the confines of an old one, or even instead of it developing in the interstitial areas between two old ones, we find new disciplines developing now which are many-parented and which originate in a great many different fields. The most striking example of the new kind of discipline is cybernetics, which comes from mathematics, electrical engineering, physiology, and even perhaps a bit from economics. The very new and somewhat ill-named discipline of "management science" draws also from a large number of different fields: from economics, from cybernetics itself, from social-psychology, and from many branches of engineering. Eiconics is clearly one of these many-parented disciplines. It does not fit, therefore, very easily into the organizational structure of departments within the academic community. It is a little difficult to visualize a dean setting up a department of eiconics or anybody endowing a chair in it. One doubts very much whether it will produce a professional society. In this respect it is certainly not a new science or a new department of knowledge. It exists, if it exists at all, precariously poised between a number of different stools and in considerable danger of falling between all of them.

It may be, nevertheless, that we are in the midst, or perhaps only at the beginning, of a profound reorganization of the departmental structure of knowledge and of academic life. The old departmental boundaries are crumbling in all directions in the physical as well as in the social sciences. There is something abroad which might be called an interdisciplinary movement. It is reflected at one level in the interest in general education. It is reflected at another level in the development of cross-disciplinary institutes, for instance, institutes of industrial relations, institutes of international relations, area studies, and so on. It is reflected at another level in the development of small groups of interested people pursuing the objective of integration of knowledge. The Encyclopaedia of Unified Science centering at Chicago, the Institute of Management Science centering at Pittsburgh, the Social Relations Department at Harvard, and the Society for the Advancement of General Systems Theory now in the process of organization are all perhaps straws in the wind. It may be, however, that what we are witnessing is not so much the unification of knowledge as its restructuring. This restructuring is being forced upon us by the very growth of knowledge itself. Now that the transcript of science has become so large that a single individual cannot hope to encompass a hundredth part of it in the course of a lifetime, the problem of order and economy in learning, that is, the transmission of the transcript into the image of the scientist, becomes of overwhelming importance. The academic world generally goes on the assumption that the more we know of everything the better. This at least seems to be the assumption that underlies the requirements for a Ph.D. The student has always known better than this. He has usually operated on the principle of knowing as little as he can get away with. It is time, perhaps, for this principle to be made respectable. We must re-examine the whole process of formal education from the point of view of what is the *minimum* knowledge, not the maximum, which must be transmitted if the whole structure is not to fall apart. Any economizing of learning, therefore, is highly desirable. Eiconics may be more of a contribution to this restructuring of the universe of knowledge than it is a new science in the sense in which the old sciences are sciences. If a single theoretical principle can be shown to apply over a wide area of the empirical world, this is economy in the learning process. Mathematics itself is, in a sense, such a body of principles; hence, its extreme importance in science. Mathematics is perhaps too general; its domain is not merely the possible but the conceivable and perhaps even the inconceivable. We are perhaps in the process of organizing a general theory of the empirical world: something which lies between the extreme generality of mathematics and the particularity of particular disciplines. I visualize eiconics as occupying a place in this theoretical structure alongside, perhaps, cybernetics. It will be a long time, of course, before the restructuring of knowledge which now seems to be underway will be reflected in the organization of the universities. Indeed, it is difficult to visualize now exactly what the appropriate organization would be. There can be little doubt, however, that, if the restructuring which I have suggested is in fact underway, it will eventually be recognized officially. Until then, the new structures, as new intellectual structures always have done, will have to live in an underworld, an underworld of deviant professors, gifted amateurs, and moderate crackpots. To this underworld, I invite my no doubt somewhat alarmed and bewildered readers.

11

The Image and Truth:
Some Philosophical Implications

IN THE THEORY
which I have put forward in these pages, I have en-
deavored to steer clear of the great philosophical issue
of epistemology, that is, of the theory of knowledge in
philosophical terms. I have considered the dynamics of
behavior in terms of what is essentially an abstraction:
the image. I have not considered the question, whether
the image is "true," or how, if it is true, we know that it
is true. I have been able to avoid these great and rather
unanswerable questions largely because what I have been
developing is an abstraction. It is the fact that it is an
abstraction which gives it some claim to be the foundation of a science rather than a philosophy. Science might
almost be defined as the process of substituting unimportant questions which can be answered for important
questions which cannot. Up to the present period of
intellectual history, the theory of knowledge has generally
been regarded as a subject for philosophy rather than
for science. What I am proposing in effect, is to make a
science out of knowledge by the deft substitution of
something that is not what the philosopher means by
knowledge, namely the image, for the real thing. It is by

these deft substitutions that science grows and philosophy is none the poorer for them. I maintain, therefore, that the theory of the image which I have put forward, or, which my critics may well observe, I have merely glimpsed from afar, is consistent with a great number of philosophical positions regarding the ultimate nature of truth and our perception of it. I do not regard myself as committed to any particular epistemology. I may be accused of stealing the image from the temple of truth, but my act in no way depends on the rite by which the image is worshipped.

It cannot be denied, however, that the view which I have been putting forward has philosophical implications and that these implications may be of some relevance to the theory itself. Within the confines of my abstraction, for instance, it is clear that the problem of truth and validity cannot be solved completely, if what we mean by the truth of an image is its correspondence with some reality in the world outside it. The difficulty with any correspondence theory of truth (as the philosophers have known for a long time) is that images can only be compared with images. They can never be compared with any outside reality. The difficulty with the coherence theory of truth, on the other hand, is that the coherence or consistency of the image is simply not what we mean by its truth. Even lies can be beautifully coherent and consistent, and even though we may argue that there is no perfect lie any more than there is a perfect crime and that some little slip or inconsistency will always find the liar out, still we cannot be sure of this. We have no real guarantee that the "outside" to which the image is supposed to correspond, is itself consistent and coherent; indeed, there are philosophers, like the existentialists, who argue that it is not, that the real world outside us is in fact a mass of inconsistencies and absurdities and is in a very real sense nonsense. The consistency and coherence which we pretend to detect in it, they argue, is merely a fashion of our own minds.

All this does not mean that we have to retreat into solipsism, that is, the doctrine that there is no reality outside the mind of the philosopher who happens to be writing. The great difficulty with solipsism is that nobody believes it. The image is universally affected with reality, that is to say, part of our image is the belief that parts of it are more real than others. Our image includes within itself, as it were, the notion that the common-sense world which we see around us is actually "there," and it certainly does not include the idea that all we see around us is an illusion. Even the Indian doctrine of Maya does not imply solipsism. The Hindu philosopher and, indeed, the modern physicist as well may argue that the world as we commonly perceive it is a result of a deeper set of causes. It is an illusion that the table, says the physicist (what philosopher could do without a table), is a solid mass; in fact, according to him, it is largely empty space inhabited by largely nonexistent electrons, or perhaps only by fields of force or mathematical equations. It does not follow, in the least, that the table is merely a structure within my image.

We are saved from solipsism partly by feedback, partly by the perception that our image is a public image. Even if we have no symbolic communication as in the famous examples of feral children, the image of the world which is built up by experience is still that of a world outside. This is because the messages which we send out from ourselves as acts return as confirming perceptions. We put out our hand to touch the table, and behold, it is stopped. The doves which we send out from our little arks return

166

with branches in their mouths. It is quite clear that even the animals inhabit as public a world as we do. With the development of symbolic messages and the building up of a public image not only by messages from nature but by messages from each other, the danger of solipsism is still further removed. The only true solipsist is the hopeless schizophrenic, the person who has cut himself off from all feedback, whether from nature or from man.

It is still necessary to inquire even within the framework of our abstract theory what we mean when we say that an image is true or is false. At various levels of discourse or enlightenment, there are a number of things which may be meant by this statement. If I say that your image is not true, I may simply mean that it is not the same as mine. This, indeed, is frequently what we mean even when we dress up the statement in elegant philosophical language. I think most of us would agree, however, that this statement of what we mean by saying that an image is true is not satisfactory simply because it does not correspond to our own image of what we think of as truth. The same objection applies, for instance, to what has been called the "boo-hurrah" school of ethics. When we say that something is bad, our image includes more than the expression, "I do not like it."

At a somewhat higher level of discourse, therefore, we may perhaps argue that when we say an image is not true, we mean that it is not the same as the public image of our subculture. A non-Catholic might argue, for instance, that this is what a Catholic means by "Catholic truth," and a nonscientist might argue similarly that this is what the scientist means by scientific truth. Here again, however, the image is not satisfactory. The proposition, "the image of my subculture may be wrong," cannot be ruled out as nonsensical. We have all changed our images

167

often enough to know that few of them can be regarded as sacred or unchangeable.

At still another level of discourse it can be argued that what we mean by the truth of an image is its survival value. This argument can take two forms. We can argue that the truth of an image is measured by the stability, that is the survival of the image itself, or we can argue that the truth of the image is measured by the ability which it confers for survival on the organism possessing it. However, it can be argued with alarming cogency that lies are frequently more stable and have a better survival value than the truth. As we have already seen, the internal stability of the image is not merely a result of its logical consistency but also a result of nonlogical factors. The image of racial superiority, for instance, is logically absurd, is inconsistent with the basic religious images held by Western peoples, and receives extremely little support from the scientific subculture. It nevertheless exhibits deplorable persistence because, perhaps, it is able to repair the rather tattered value image of the individual holding it. It might almost be said, indeed, that the most stable images are those which are least susceptible to feedback. The transempirical images which we do not even pretend to confirm by experience are perhaps the most stable of all.

We cannot claim either that the ability of an image to contribute to the survival of the individual possessing it is a satisfactory image of truth. If there is a tiger in the room (in the image, of course, of an impartial observer well outside the room) the man who doesn't see it is just about as well off as the man who does. Indeed, it may well be that the man who doesn't see the tiger has the best chance of survival. He will not be paralyzed with fear, he will not attract the tiger's attention, and by going about his own business quietly, he may escape the destruction which his more knowing fellow invites by the very effects of his knowledge. We cannot rule out the possibility that under some circumstances, ignorance is bliss, and knowledge leads to disaster. It is still a moot question, unfortunately, whether the development of large and complex images closely approximating to the "truth," as in man, is, indeed, very good for survival. The slightly chilling remark that man may be an unsuccessful experiment in curiosity veers a little too close to the cold winds of reality for comfort. One wonders, sometimes, whether the occasional appearance of new stars in the firmament does not represent certain unanticipated consequences of the discovery of atomic energy by intelligent beings. We have now reached the point in human development where the end of the earth brought about by human knowledge is a real possibility. Curiously enough, however, our very inability to survive would be remarkably good evidence for the truth of our images—if anybody was there to notice it.

At still another level, we may argue that what we mean by truth, or at least the progress toward truth, is an orderly development of the image, especially of the public and transcribed image through its confirmation by feedback messages. This in a sense is the philosophy of science. Truth ever eludes our grasp, but we are always moving asymptotically toward it. Out of our image we predict the messages which will return to us as a result of our acts. If this prediction is fulfilled the image is confirmed, if it is not fulfilled the image must be changed. This is the essence of the logical-positivist view that definitions must be operational and hypotheses must be testable. Science in this view is a sort of grand extension of domestic science. All textbooks should be recipe books, and the proof of the recipe, like that of the pudding, is in the eating. The operational definition of validity would seem to be the writing of an article in the learned journals from which there is neither backfire, stomach-ache, or head-ache. Unfortunately, this definition applies just as well to an article that nobody reads as to an article that no-body criticizes.

The difficulty with the "orderly development" view of validation, of which logical positivism is one form, is that there are so many examples of such orderly develop-ments, many of which are inconsistent with one another. The history of Catholic dogma represents an orderly de-velopment with modification of an image according to an extensive system of feedbacks quite as much as does the development of scientific doctrine. Suppose, for in-stance, that the hypothesis is suggested that the sacred heart of Jesus is a suitable and a rewarding object of devo-tion. The hypothesis is tested by trying it out. People try this devotion and are suitably rewarded by both visi-ble and invisible marks of divine favor, and the doctrine eventually becomes an accepted part of the transcript of the Church. The process is surely all that any logical posi-tivist could desire, yet most of them would probably be loath to accept it into the Olympus of scientific respect-ability.

At still another level, we may argue that truth is some-thing which comes to us with authority. It is part of our image of society that there are some people who know things and some people who don't. The problem of truth, therefore, is to find the people who know things and to listen to them. This image may not actually be far from the image of primitive man. In the mind of the primitive, truth is what the wise men of the tribe know. They in-herited it from their forefathers and they brought the message on to their descendants. There are many survivals of this point of view in our own society. Our very ceremonial trappings go back to it: the gown of the scholar, the robe of the judge, the uniform of the general, and the vestments of the priest clothe not only their wearers with pomp but the messages that flow from them with authority. We may feel that science has emancipated us from this dependence on authority and that the messages of science come clothed with their own authority alone, not with the authority of the speaker. This is, no doubt, the ideal. In practice, however, there is so little possibility for direct confirmation of most of the images of science on the part of their recipients that authority again clothes the words of wisdom. The graduate student who confirms, in a new way, the images of the professors is praised for his originality. The one who denies the sacred images will, in general, not be awarded his degree. We shall delude ourselves if we think that the self-perpetuation of images through the apostolic succession of authority is unknown to science.

The question must be faced, therefore, whether the theory of the image does not move us in the direction of a philosophical skepticism more devastating even than that of Hume. The acid of science which has eaten away so many ancient images now is seen to turn on the image of science itself. The white-coated high priest of truth: austere, objective, operational, realistic, validating, is degraded to the status of the servant of a subculture, trapped in the fortress of its own defended public image, and straining the grains of truth through its own value system. As the physicist dissolves the hard table into whirling atoms, so the communication and information theorist dissolves the hard fact into messages filtered through a value system. Like Hume, we pale before the abyss of skepticism toward which our logic leads us relentlessly, but from which we draw back horrified, incredulous at incredulity. Like Hume, also, we go off and have a good dinner and then we feel better. We put philosophy into the back of the filing cabinet and shut it tight and return to the cheerful and ordinary business of life "believing where we cannot prove." From the abyss of reason we turn again to clutch at the slender rope of faith.

Faith, yes, but what faith? To this question, of course, the theory of the image gives no answer. We can only say that there are elements in the image which are capable of organizing the life and activity of the individual. It is these organizing elements which constitute faith: the faith of the experimental scientist in his method; the faith of the believer in his God; the faith of the crusader in his cause; the faith of the soldier in his nation, or perhaps only in his buddies. All these are organizing images. Their origins are obscure and their consequences are profound. Where life is disorganized, where there is dissatisfaction and discontent with the processes of existing faith, then there is search for change. Where a faith is discovered that has this organizing power, it is likely to grow and to prosper. In our present state of knowledge, however, we must confess that the sources of organizing power are mysterious. Faiths are the genes of society. Their operation is as potent and as mysterious as that of the gene in biology.

I have argued that eiconics as an abstract discipline is consistent with a great many metaphysical or epistemological viewpoints. We can study the formation of images, the impact of messages, and the consequences of images for behavior without committing ourselves to any tests of ultimate validity. Just as two negatives make a positive, so having illusions about an illusion would seem to be almost the same process as finding out the truth about truth. Nevertheless, there are certain issues of a more or less philosophical nature which can, I think, be sharply illuminated by the theory of the image. One of these is the famous discussion regarding the relation of facts and values: a discussion which has been going on probably since the very beginnings of philosophy. The theory of the image is distinctly unfriendly to the position that facts and values are quite distinct, that facts are a proper subject for scientific study, whereas values are not, that facts are objective and values are subjective. In the theory of the image, images of fact and images of value are alike present in the image. The question at issue is whether the formation of these two aspects or dimensions of the image follows different principles. Is the process by which we build up our image of the factual or relational world, for instance, essentially different from the process by which we build up an image of the value ordering of this world? I would argue strongly that these two processes, though there may be some differences between them, are essentially similar. The raw material of our image, both of fact and of value, is messages. It may be, of course, that symbolic and internal messages may play a larger part in establishing our image of value, and that messages from nature play a larger part in establishing our image of fact. Even this proposition, however, could be questioned. By far the greater part of our image of fact is built up from symbolic messages from some transcript or from some teacher. Even images as factual as our images of space and time, for instance, that is, of geography and history, are built up almost entirely from symbolic messages. In most of the people of the world, the image of Australia as a fact is built up entirely by symbolic messages. For all of us the image of Henry VIII is built up by symbolic messages. Some people now alive have seen Australia; nobody now alive has seen Henry VIII. Our relational images, likewise, are built up largely by symbolic messages, not by messages from nature. Similarly, it can be argued that our value images are built up just like our images of fact by a combination of symbolic messages and messages from nature. The value structure begins with simple pain or pleasure—messages from nature that have strong value connotations. As the relational image develops, the early value structure grows and begins to cover a large part of the image field. Symbolic and charismatic messages are, of course, important in its development, but perhaps no more so than they are in the development of our image of fact.

What, perhaps, is even more destructive to the view that makes a sharp distinction between facts and values is that according to the theory of the image, our very message input depends to a considerable extent upon our existing value structure. What this means, in a sense, is that the way in which the total image grows determines or at least limits the directions of future growth. In this growth process, however, the factual and the valuational images are inextricably entwined. The distinction between messages from nature and symbolic messages is a vital one; the distinction between facts and values is not. One important consequence of this position is that values are now seen to be just as appropriate a subject of "scientific inquiry" as facts. This is not to say that values can be validated by scientific inquiry, but then neither can facts be so validated. We can examine consistency, coherence, survival value, stability, and organizing power in the image, because the image can investigate the image. We can never examine the correspondence of the image with reality, whether in the field of value or in the field of fact.

Although eiconics as an abstract discipline falls firmly within the subculture of science and is committed to no particular philosophical position, nevertheless, because no part of the image is really independent of any other part, eiconics at least points toward certain philosophical positions with which it is most comfortable. It leads in the direction of a broad, eclectic, organic, yet humble epistemology looking for processes of organization rather than specific tests of validity and finding these processes in many areas of life and experience: in art, religion, and in the common experiences of daily life, as well as in science. It is least friendly to those philosophical positions which put all the eggs of truth in one basket of method, whether that of experiment or of revelation. It seeks truth in a way and a life, or perhaps, in many ways and in many lives. It emphasizes communication and feedback as the great sources for orderly and organized growth; thus linking hands with both cybernetics and semantics. Most of all, perhaps, it brings the actor into the act; it looks beyond mechanism without falling into vitalism. It represents, I hope, one small step toward the unknown goal of human history.

Selected Ann Arbor Paperbacks
Works of enduring merit

For a complete list of Ann Arbor Paperback titles write:
THE UNIVERSITY OF MICHIGAN PRESS ANN ARBOR